CW01108738

Kids' Cookbook

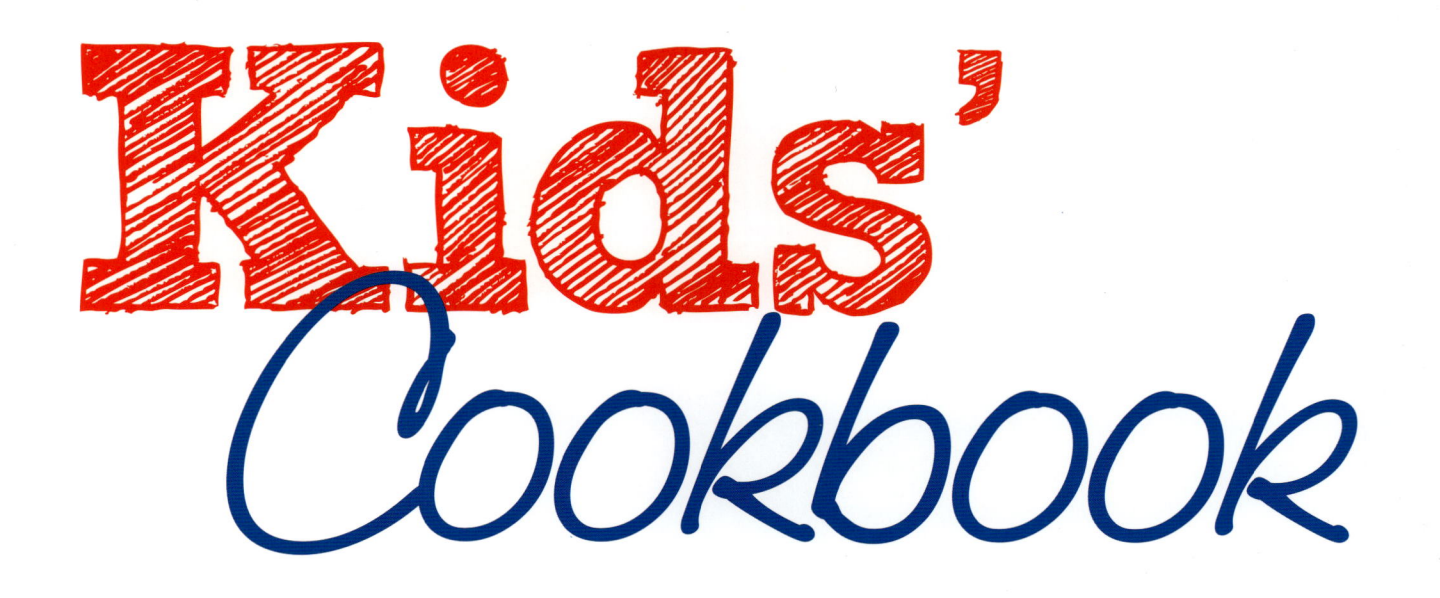

The Confident Cooking Promise of Success

Welcome to the world of Confident Cooking, where recipes are triple-tested by a team of home economists to achieve a high standard of success—and delicious results every time.

bay books

The Publisher thanks the following for their assistance:

Accoutrement Cookshops
Butler and Co. Kitchen Homewares
Corso De'Fiori
House & Garden
Anna Marchant
Mosmania
My Shop Ceramics
Linden and Sheridan Pride
St John Ambulance
Villeroy and Boch

All recipes in this book can be made by a child with little or no help from an adult. Microwave recipes have been tested in a 600–700 watt microwave. Each recipe is set out to make cooking simple.

EASY
MEDIUM
HARD

Recipes are graded to help you learn. If you are just starting out to cook you might prefer to try the recipes marked easy (1 chef's hat); when you have a little experience, try medium (2 chefs' hats) and when you are more experienced try hard (3 chefs' hats) recipes.

CONTENTS

GETTING STARTED
Hints and tips to make cooking easy, cooking terms and the measuring of ingredients fully explained.   6

CHAPTER ONE
SNACKS AND DRINKS
Perfect for those in-between times   12

CHAPTER TWO
VEGETABLES AND SALADS
Crisp and crunchy vegetables and salads that taste terrific   24

CHAPTER THREE
CHICKEN, SEAFOOD AND MEAT
Main dishes that taste a treat   36

WAKE-UP BREAKFAST TRAY
How to treat Mum and Dad with a special breakfast tray   50

CHAPTER FOUR
PIES, PASTA AND PIZZA
Quick, easy and fun to make   52

CHAPTER FIVE
MICROWAVE COOKERY
Microwave versions of some sweet and savoury favourites   60

CHAPTER SIX
DESSERTS
Scrumptious desserts that make a perfect finish for your meal   72

CHAPTER SEVEN
CAKES
Super-yummy cakes, easy to make and easy to eat   86

GIFTS FROM THE KITCHEN
Home-made gifts to celebrate birthdays and special occasions   94

CHAPTER EIGHT
COOKIES AND SLICES
Assorted sweet treats to enjoy any time   96

USEFUL INFORMATION   109

INDEX   110

GETTING STARTED

Cooking is great fun but before you start, take time to get organised. Read over the recipe thoroughly, read it all the way through and check that you have all the ingredients. Collect everything you need for your recipe — all the ingredients and all the equipment.

If you need to use the oven for baking, turn it on to the correct temperature before you start the recipe. Arrange the oven shelves at the height you want before turning the oven on.

If your recipe calls for chopped or shredded ingredients do this before you begin. Also open any cans and wash any vegetables or fruits. Grease any baking tins if you need to.

All the recipes are set out in easy to follow step-by-step form. Remember to finish each step before beginning the next one.

IMPORTANT SAFETY POINTS

Here are a few hints and tips to make cooking safe and enjoyable.

✔ Always ask an adult for permission before you start.
✔ Before starting to cook, wash your hands well with soap and water. Wear an apron to protect your clothes and wear closed-in, non-slip shoes to protect your feet.
✔ Collect everything you need for your recipe before you start — all the ingredients and the necessary kitchen equipment.
✔ Unless you are allowed to use knives, ask an adult to help you chop things. Never cut directly on a kitchen surface — always use a chopping board. When you are using a knife pick it up by the handle, not by the blade. Keep your fingers well clear of the blade when chopping foods.
✔ Take care when washing knives, too. Keep the sharp edge of the blade away from you and store the knives out of reach of any young brothers or sisters.
✔ Always use oven gloves when you are moving anything into or out of the oven. Remember that anything you take from the oven or from the stove top will stay hot for a while.
✔ Turn saucepan handles to the side when cooking so you don't knock them. Remember to hold the handles of saucepans when stirring foods on the stove and use a wooden spoon or a metal spoon with a wooden handle. (All metal spoons can get hot when stirring foods.)
✔ Place hot saucepans and ovenproof dishes on a chopping board when you take them from the oven or the stove. Never set a hot pan directly on the kitchen bench or table, unless it is covered with ceramic tiles.
✔ Never use electrical appliances near water. Always have dry hands before you start to use any appliance.
✔ Be very careful with pots and pans on the stove. Never reach across a hot saucepan of food — steam is very hot and can cause a nasty burn.
✔ Remember to turn off the oven, the hotplate or gas ring or any other appliance when you have finished using it.
✔ Most importantly, clean up the kitchen when you have finished cooking. Put away all the ingredients and the equipment you have used. Wash the dishes — start with washing the least soiled dishes like glassware and bowls and then do the messy pans and baking tins. Dry the dishes thoroughly and put them back in their place. Wipe down your work surface with a clean cloth and then, I'm sure, you'll be allowed to cook again another day.

First Aid for Burns and Scalds

Cool the burnt parts with cold water for at least ten minutes. Make the hurt person comfortable, but do not move them if the burn or scald is serious. Protect against infection by covering the burns or scalds with clean non-adherent material. Do not touch. Do not remove stuck clothing.

If someone's clothing catches fire approach holding a rug, blanket or coat in front of yourself. Wrap it around the person and lay them flat. Smother the flames.

If anyone is seriously hurt, ring for an ambulance.

COOK'S TOOLS

There are many tools used in the kitchen to make cooking easy. There are wooden and metal spoons to stir with, spatulas to combine ingredients, bowls of varying sizes to mix things in, strainers or colanders to drain and rinse foods in, and a whole array of different size saucepans and baking trays to cook things in. Then there are wire racks for cooling cakes and cookies, metal spatulas to help you measure and also to spread ingredients or toppings evenly over foods.

The recipes in this book use only basic equipment found in most kitchens. If in doubt about any equipment you may need to ask an adult for some help.

GETTING STARTED

SOME SIMPLE COOKING TERMS

BEAT: to stir foods with a spoon or electric mixer until they are smooth.

BOILING POINT: when a liquid bubbles in a steady pattern and the bubbles break on the surface; steam also starts to rise from the pan.

CHOP: to cut food carefully into small pieces. To chop finely is to cut foods as small as you can.

DRAIN: to strain away unwanted liquid using a colander or strainer, as when you have cooked spaghetti. Do this over the kitchen sink so that water can drain away down the sink. Ask an adult for help, as a large pan of water can be very heavy.

GRATE: to rub food against a grater. Do this over kitchen paper. Hold the grater with one hand and rub the food back and forth over the grating holes. This gives you long thin pieces. For finely grated foods use the smallest grating holes.

GREASE: to rub baking tins and cooking utensils with butter, margarine or oil to stop foods sticking when you bake them.

MASH: to squash cooked or very ripe foods with a fork or potato masher.

SEPARATING EGGS: for making use of egg whites or yolks. Hold the egg over a small plate and carefully crack the shell with a metal spatula or table knife. Let the egg fall out onto the plate, place a small glass over the yolk and then carefully tip the white into a bowl. If any yolk gets into the white, you can easily remove it with a piece of eggshell.

SIMMER: to cook food over a very low heat so that only a few bubbles appear over the surface. When a recipe calls for food to boil and then simmer, simply turn the heat down to the lowest setting.

SLICE: to cut foods like apples, carrots and tomatoes into thin rounds or sections.

STIR: to combine ingredients by stirring them together in a bowl or saucepan.

COOKED INGREDIENTS

Some of the recipes in this book call for cooked rice, pasta, vegetables and mashed vegetables. If you don't have any of these cooked foods as leftovers in your refrigerator you will need to prepare them before you start your recipe. Follow these guidelines and if in doubt ask for adult help.

TO COOK RICE AND PASTA
Firstly you will need to put a large saucepan of water on to boil. (Use 2 L water for 500 g pasta.) Add 1 tablespoon of oil to the water. For 2½ cups of cooked rice or pasta you will need 1 cup uncooked rice or pasta. Add the rice or pasta to the steadily boiling water, stir in carefully and cook for 8–12 minutes or until tender. You may need to ask an adult to help you drain it in a colander or strainer over the sink because a large pot of water can be very heavy. Use the rice or pasta immediately for hot dishes or rinse well with cold water and cool for cold dishes.

Add oil to boiling water.

Add pasta to boiling water; stir.

TO COOK VEGETABLES
Wash vegetables, trim if necessary and cut into required shape. Put a large saucepan of water on to boil, and when boiling very carefully lower vegetables into water. Cook until vegetables are just tender. If in doubt ask an adult to help you test your vegetables for doneness, and then ask them to assist you with draining them.

For mashed potatoes or pumpkin it is best to cook them a little longer until soft and then drain them. Place them in a bowl and use a potato masher or fork to squash them to a mushy consistency.

Cut into even-sized pieces.

Drain vegetables using a colander.

Mash with a vegetable masher.

GETTING STARTED

MEASURING UP

Careful measuring of your ingredients makes for a successful recipe. You will need a set of dry measuring cups, which usually come in a set of four: a 1 cup measure, $\frac{1}{2}$ cup, $\frac{1}{3}$ cup and $\frac{1}{4}$ cup measure. These are used to measure ingredients like flour and sugar. You will also need a liquid measuring cup that usually has a lip for easy pouring and lines on the side that mark the different liquid measures. Milk, water and juice are measured with this cup. Measuring spoons will also be needed to measure small amounts. They are marked and measure 1 tablespoon, 1 teaspoon, $\frac{1}{2}$ teaspoon and $\frac{1}{4}$ teaspoon.

LIQUID MEASURES

To measure a liquid ingredient place the liquid measuring cup on the bench or board, add some of the liquid and bend down so that your eyes are level with the measurement marks. Check to see if you have enough liquid; if necessary pour in a little more. If you have too much liquid simply pour out the extra.

DRY MEASURES

Take care to use the correct size measuring cup as stated in the recipe, especially if you are baking cakes or cookies. Spoon the dry ingredients lightly into the measuring cup and level it off with a metal spatula. It's a good idea to do this over a bowl or a piece of grease proof paper to avoid any mess.

In some recipes you will need to do some simple maths to get the correct amount you need. For example you may need $\frac{2}{3}$ cup flour for a recipe, so simply measure out $\frac{1}{3}$ cup using the correct measure and then another $\frac{1}{3}$ cup and add both to the recipe.

Brown sugar is measured as a dry ingredient and you will need to pack it down tightly in the measuring cup, filling it until it is level with the top of the cup. You will probably find that you need to run a metal spatula around the cup to loosen the sugar.

SPOON MEASURES

Measuring spoons are different from the spoons you use for eating. They are used to measure small amounts.

To measure liquid choose the correct size spoon for the amount you need and carefully pour the liquid into the bowl of the spoon. It's a good idea to hold the spoon over a cup or jug to avoid spills.

To measure dry ingredients fill the correct spoon with your dry ingredients and then carefully level off the amount with a metal spatula.

BUTTER AND MARGARINE

Butter and margarine are generally measured in grams. You will find that blocks of butter have a weight marking on the side of the wrapper. Use a small knife to cut through the butter at the correct marking and then unwrap it. Butter and margarine may also be weighed using a kitchen scale.

CHAPTER ONE
SNACKS AND DRINKS

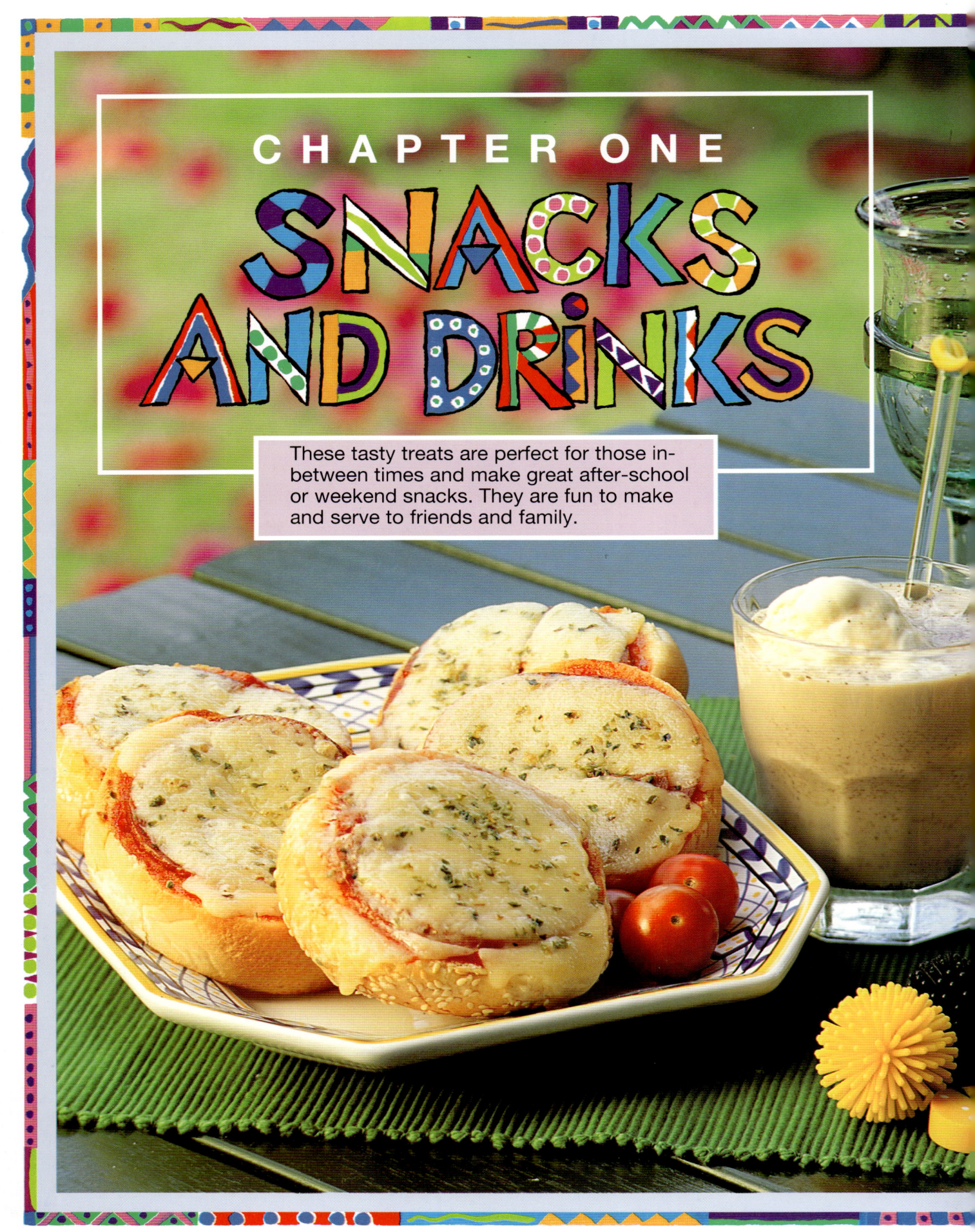

These tasty treats are perfect for those in-between times and make great after-school or weekend snacks. They are fun to make and serve to friends and family.

13

CHEESE TOAST

Serves 6

1 cup grated Cheddar cheese
2 tablespoons chutney
1 tablespoon grated onion
1 tablespoon tomato sauce
1 teaspoon Worcestershire sauce
25 g butter
6 thick slices wholegrain bread

1. Put the grated cheese into a mixing bowl.
2. Add chutney, onion, tomato sauce + Worcestershire sauce.
3. Melt butter in small pan. Stir in to mixing bowl.
4. Turn the grill on to high.
5. Toast the bread on one side only.
6. Spread cheese mixture on untoasted side.
7. Put it back under grill until cheese is melted.
8. Slice and serve it straight away.

Before the days of the pop-up toaster, you made toast by holding the bread up to the fire on a long-handled toasting fork. Smoked toast and charred fingers were often the result.

CINNAMON TOAST

Serves 6

6 tablespoons caster sugar
2 tablespoons cinnamon
6 thick slices bread
softened butter

1. Put the sugar into a small jar or cup.
2. Add the cinnamon and stir until mixed.
3. Put the bread in toaster.
4. Toast it until golden.
5. Butter toast immediately.
6. Sprinkle cinnamon and sugar evenly over.
7. Slice the toast + serve.
8. Put lid on jar and use any leftover cinnamon + sugar any time.

GARLIC TOAST

Serves 4

25 g butter
½ teaspoon garlic salt
6 thin slices wholegrain bread

1. Turn oven to 150°C (300°F)
2. Melt the butter.
3. Mix in the garlic.
4. Brush it on each piece of bread.
5. Cut each piece of bread into 3 strips.
6. Put (butter side up) on to an oven sheet.
7. Bake for 30 minutes.
8. Serve hot with soup.

ONION DIP

Serves 6–8

1 x 45 g packet of dried French onion-style soup
2 tablespoons vinegar
¾ cup softened cream cheese
1 cup plain yoghurt
¼ cup chopped parsley

1. Empty packet of soup into small bowl.
2. Add vinegar. Stir it a little.
3. Put it aside for about 30 minutes.
4. Stir in cream cheese.
5. Stir in the yoghurt stirring it all well.
6. Stir in the parsley. Put a lid on bowl.
7. Put in fridge until needed.
8. Put on a serving plate with crackers on chips.

PIZZA SNACKS

Serves 4

2 hamburger buns
30 g butter, melted
¼ cup tomato sauce
12 thin slices of salami
8 thin slices of cheese (about 5 x 2 cm)
1 teaspoon dried oregano

1. Cut the hamburger buns in half.
2. Brush the 4 halves with melted butter.
3. Toast lightly under grill. Leave the grill on.
4. Brush toasted halves with tomato sauce.
5. Top each half with 3 slices of salami.
6. Put 2 slices of cheese on top of each.
7. Sprinkle a little oregano on top.
8. Put back under grill till cheese is bubbly.

19

COFFEE FLOAT

Serves 6

- 2 tablespoons instant coffee powder
- 2 tablespoons sugar
- 3/4 cup hot water
- 1 teaspoon vanilla essence
- 4 cups cold milk
- 6 scoops vanilla ice-cream
- cocoa powder, to sprinkle

1. Dissolve coffee and sugar in the hot water.
2. Pour into a bowl. Add the vanilla essence and milk.
3. Stir it all well.
4. Chill in the fridge until it's very cold.
5. Whisk until it's foamy.
6. Put a scoop of ice-cream into 6 tall glasses.
7. Fill each glass with mixture.
8. Sprinkle with a little cocoa powder. Pop in a straw and serve.

BANANA MILKSHAKE

Serves 3

1½ cups milk
1 medium-sized banana
1 tablespoon honey
1 egg
2 tablespoons banana-flavoured yoghurt
2 scoops vanilla ice-cream
2 ice cubes

1. Pour milk into blender.
2. Peel the banana.
3. Chop up the banana. Add it to the blender.
4. Add the honey, egg and banana yoghurt.
5. Add ice cream + ice.
6. Put lid on blender. Blend well until smooth.
7. Pour it into 3 glasses.
8. Pop in straws + serve.

LEMON CORDIAL

Makes 1 litre

4 large lemons
4 cups sugar
2 cups water
2 teaspoons citric acid
1 teaspoon lemon essence

1. Squeeze juice from lemons (You'll get about 1 cup juice).
2. Put juice into a large saucepan. Add the sugar.
3. Add water + citric acid.
4. Bring it to the boil.
5. Boil 10 minutes. BE CAREFUL IT DOESN'T BOIL OVER! (MEDIUM HEAT)
6. Set it aside to cool.
7. Stir in the lemon essence.
8. Pour into 2 sterilised bottles with lids. Mix with lemonade or water to drink.

FRUIT PUNCH

Serves 10

1.25 L canned orange juice
425 g can fruit salad
1 orange
1 lemon
750 mL bottle of lemonade (chilled)

1. Pour the can of juice into a large bowl or jug.
2. Add the whole can of fruit salad.
3. Squeeze juice from orange
4. Pour it into bowl.
5. Squeeze juice from lemon. Add it to bowl.
6. Put in the fridge until it's really cold.
7. Just before serving, add the lemonade.
8. Stir it and then serve it.

CHAPTER TWO
VEGETABLES AND SALADS

A host of fresh, crisp vegetables and salads, perfect partners to main meals. Try our zesty Mixed Salad, refreshing Tomato Salad or Corn Fritters.

25

BEAN SALAD

Serves 6

1 cup sliced cooked green beans, well drained
1 cup canned whole kernel corn, well drained
1 x 310 g can red kidney beans
¼ teaspoon sugar
¼ cup oil
¼ cup white vinegar
sprinkle of salt and pepper

Diner: Waiter, what is this fly doing in my soup?
Waiter: The backstroke.

1. Put the drained green beans in a flat dish or bowl.
2. Add the drained corn. Stir it through.
3. Open can of kidney beans. Drain them well.
4. Add them to the dish.
5. Mix sugar, oil, vinegar well till sugar is dissolved.
6. Add salt and pepper. Stir well. 
7. Pour it all over beans + corn in the dish.
8. Stir through. Chill in fridge and serve.

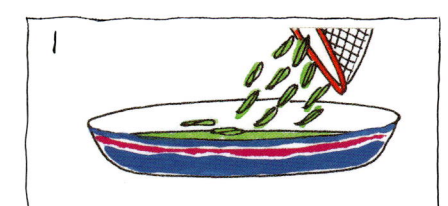

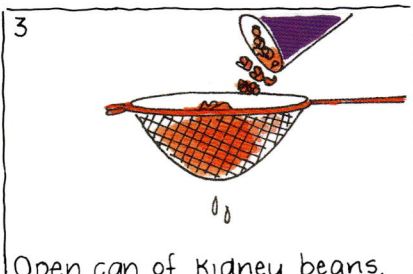

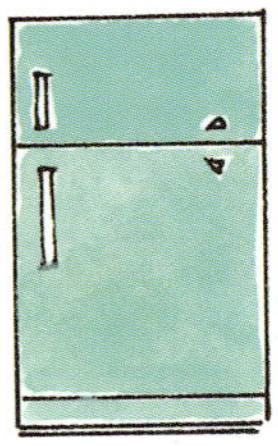

POTATO SALAD

Serves 6

6 medium potatoes
1 x 310 g can whole kernel corn
¼ cup chopped parsley
sprinkle of salt and pepper
1 tablespoon bottled French dressing
¼ cup mayonnaise

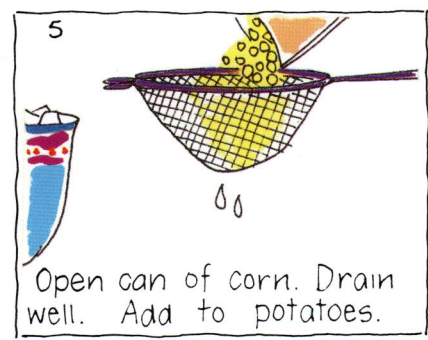

1. Scrub the potatoes until they are clean.
2. Boil them in water until tender.
3. When cool, peel them and cut into cubes.
4. Put cubes into a nice salad bowl.
5. Open can of corn. Drain well. Add to potatoes.
6. Add the parsley, the salt and the pepper.
7. Stir in French dressing and the mayonnaise.
8. Gently mix it all and serve cold.

COLESLAW

Serves 6

DRESSING
¾ cup evaporated milk
1 teaspoon sugar
¼ cup white vinegar
1 egg
sprinkle of salt and pepper

half a nice cabbage
2 medium carrots

1. Put milk, sugar, vinegar in a small saucepan.
2. Add egg, salt + pepper. Beat it till smooth.
3. Cook, stirring all the time, till it becomes thick.
4. Leave to cool. Pour into a jar and refrigerate.
5. Shred cabbage finely with a sharp knife.
6. Keep going carefully till you have 3 cupfuls.
7. Grate carrots. Toss with cabbage in salad bowl.
8. Toss with about ¾ cup of the dressing. Serves 6 people.

TOMATO SALAD

Serves 6

4 medium-sized ripe tomatoes

DRESSING
¼ cup oil
¼ cup white wine vinegar
¼ teaspoon French mustard
1 teaspoon caster sugar
cracked black pepper

> Knock, knock.
> Who's there?
> Freeze.
> Freeze who?
> Freeze a jolly good fellow!

1. Wash and dry tomatoes. Slice them thinly.
2. Arrange them in a shallow dish.
3. Put the oil, vinegar, mustard and sugar in a jar with a screw-top.
4. Mix them all together by turning the jar upside-down. Make sure the lid is on tightly!
5. Pour the dressing evenly over the tomatoes.
6. Grind some black pepper over the salad using a pepper grinder, if you have one.
7. Cover. Chill in fridge for 1 hour, then serve.
8. You could try a different dressing: Mix ¼ cup peanut oil, 2 tablespoons lemon juice, 2 teaspoons soft brown sugar and 1 tablespoon chopped fresh basil.

MIXED SALAD

Serves 6

- 8 button mushrooms
- 1 tablespoon chopped parsley
- 2 teaspoons lemon juice
- 2 tablespoons oil
- 3 zucchini
- 1 green capsicum
- 4 small tomatoes
- 5 leaves of mint
- ¼ cup bottled French dressing
- freshly ground black pepper

1. Wipe mushrooms clean. Slice them up thinly.
2. Put in bowl. Add parsley, lemon juice and oil.
3. Slice zucchini. Boil them in water for 1 minute.
4. Drain well. Rinse in cold water. Drain them again.
5. Chop the green capsicum up very finely.
6. Chop the tomatoes up into cubes. Chop up mint.
7. Put it all in a salad bowl. Stir in the mushrooms.
8. Pour French dressing over. Add pepper. Stir gently. Chill till cold and serve.

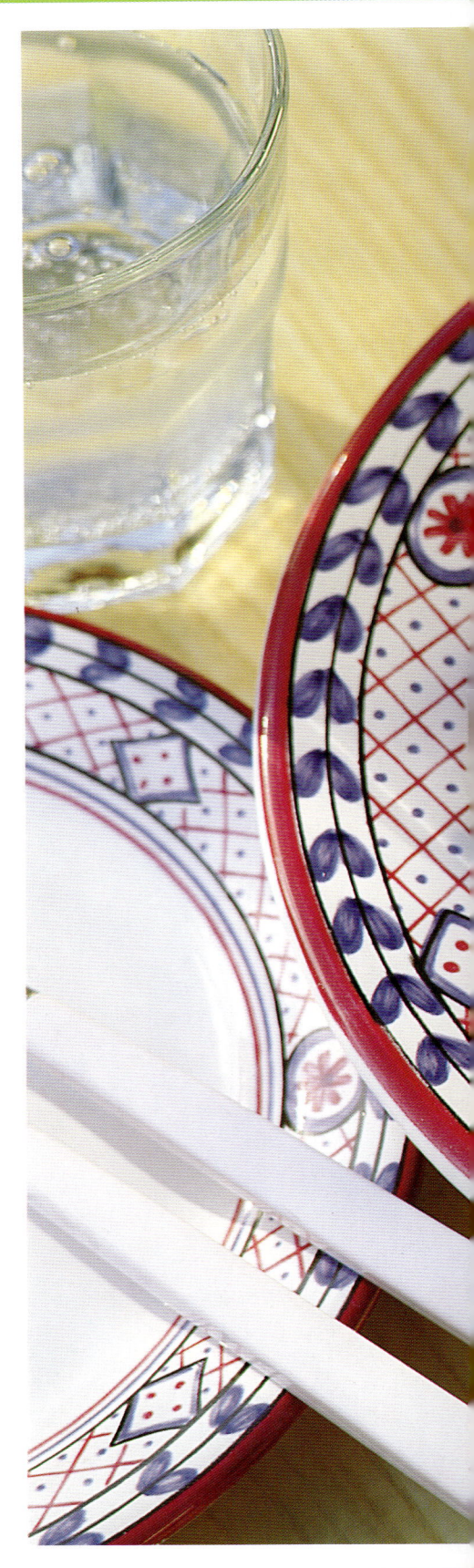

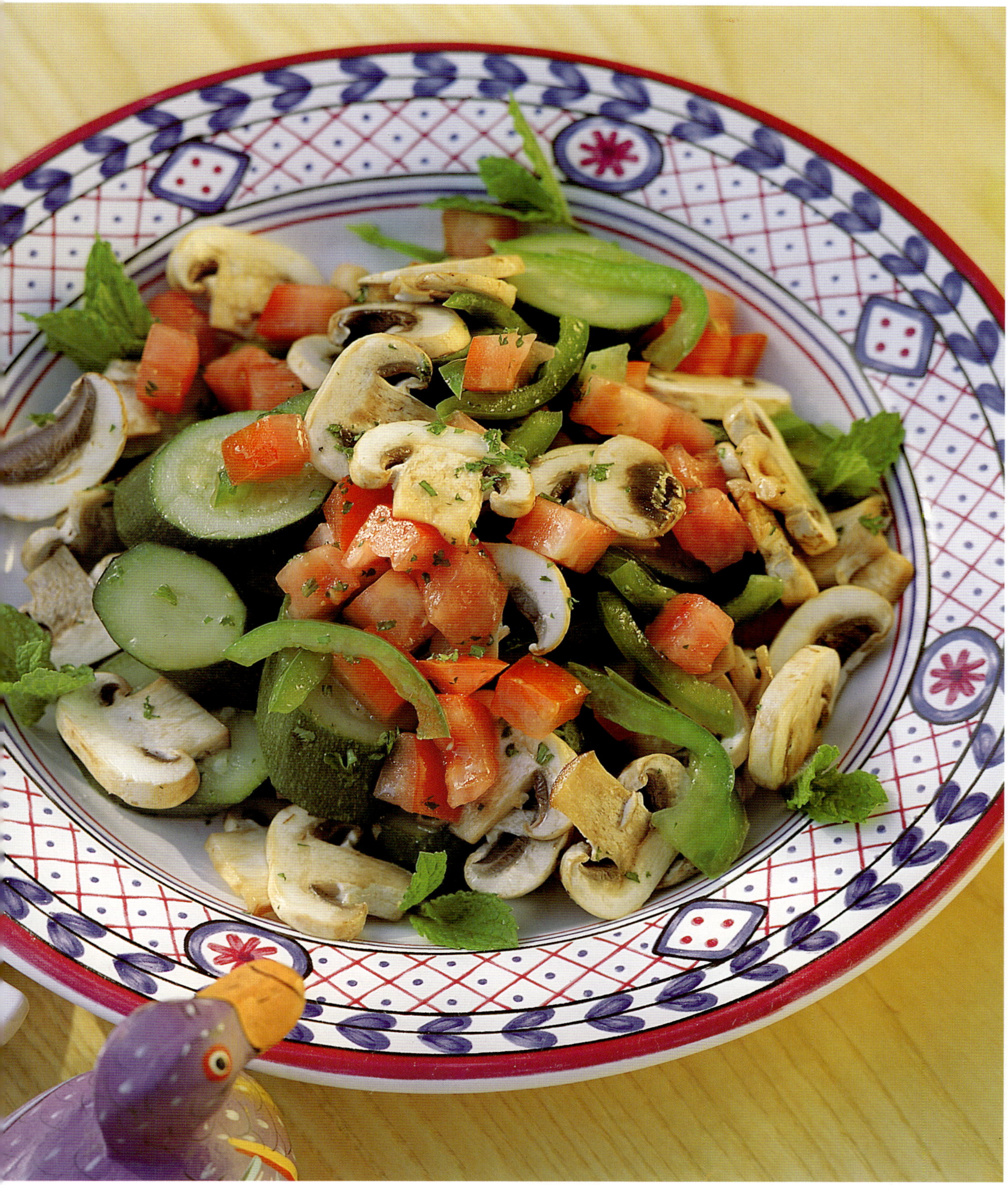

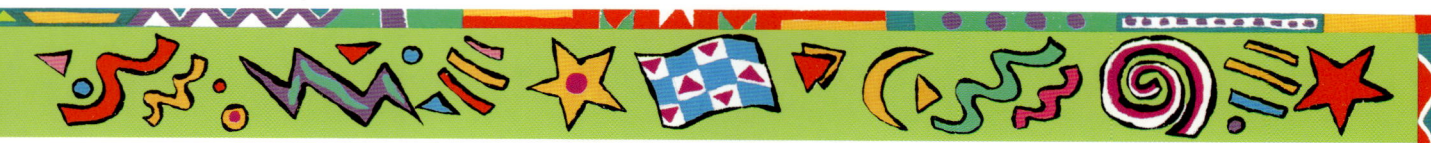

GLAZED PUMPKIN

Serves 6

750 g pumpkin
salt and pepper
50 g butter
2 tablespoons golden syrup
½ cup fresh breadcrumbs

1. Turn oven to 180°C (350°F). Grease a shallow baking dish.
2. Slice pieces of pumpkin about 3 cm thick. Trim off skin.
3. Arrange pieces in the baking dish.
4. Sprinkle pieces with salt and pepper.
5. Cover with a lid of foil. Bake for 35 minutes.
6. Melt butter + golden syrup. Stir in breadcrumbs.
7. Take foil lid off. Pour crumb mixture all over pumpkin.
8. Bake it (uncovered) for 20 minutes more.

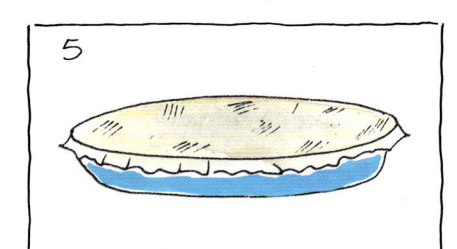

ONION AND TOMATO

Serves 4

4 medium-sized onions
3 cups water
1 medium-sized tomato
sprinkle of salt and pepper
2 tablespoons cornflour
¼ cup cold water

1. Peel onions. Slice them into rings. Put in pan.

2. Add water. Bring to the boil. Simmer 20 minutes.

3. Drain off the liquid — save ¾ cup of it.

4. Slice tomato thinly. Add to onion with the liquid.

5. Add salt and pepper. Simmer 5 minutes.

6. Mix cornflour + cold water in a cup until smooth.

7. Gently stir it in until it comes to the boil.

8. Delicious served on fish or with steak.

CORN FRITTERS

Serves 4

- 1 x 310 g can whole kernel corn
- 2 eggs
- sprinkle of salt and pepper
- ½ cup plain flour
- 1 teaspoon baking powder
- ¼ cup grated cheese
- 25 g butter
- 2 tablespoons oil

1. Drain corn. Discard liquid.
2. Put eggs, salt + pepper in a bowl. Beat well.
3. Add flour + baking powder. Whisk until smooth.
4. Add drained corn and grated cheese. Stir.
5. Put butter + oil in frypan. Heat until bubbly. MEDIUM HEAT
6. Drop spoonsful of the mixture in. MEDIUM HEAT
7. When golden, turn over and cook other side.
8. Drain on absorbent paper and serve.

SAVOURY RICE

Serves 6

- 1 tablespoon oil
- 1 onion, chopped
- 1 x 425 g can peeled tomato pieces (and the juice)
- 1 teaspoon instant chicken stock powder
- sprinkle of salt and pepper
- ¼ teaspoon sugar
- 1 x 310 g can whole kernel corn
- 3½ cups cooked rice
- 1 cup frozen peas
- 1 cup grated Cheddar cheese

> I eat my peas with honey —
> I've done it all my life.
> It makes them taste quite funny
> But it keeps them on the knife.

1. Turn oven to 180°C. (350°F) Grease an ovenproof dish.
2. Heat oil in a pan. Add onion. Fry gently.
3. Add tomatoes, stock, salt, pepper and sugar.
4. Stir it over low heat for 7 minutes.
5. Drain corn. Mix in a bowl with rice + peas.
6. Spread rice, corn and peas in the dish.
7. Pour tomato mixture over rice.
8. Sprinkle cheese over. Bake for 30 minutes.

CHAPTER THREE
CHICKEN, SEAFOOD AND MEAT

Impress your family with Chicken and Ginger, Salmon Mornay or Sweet and Sour Meatballs or any of our other recipes that are sure to have them asking for more.

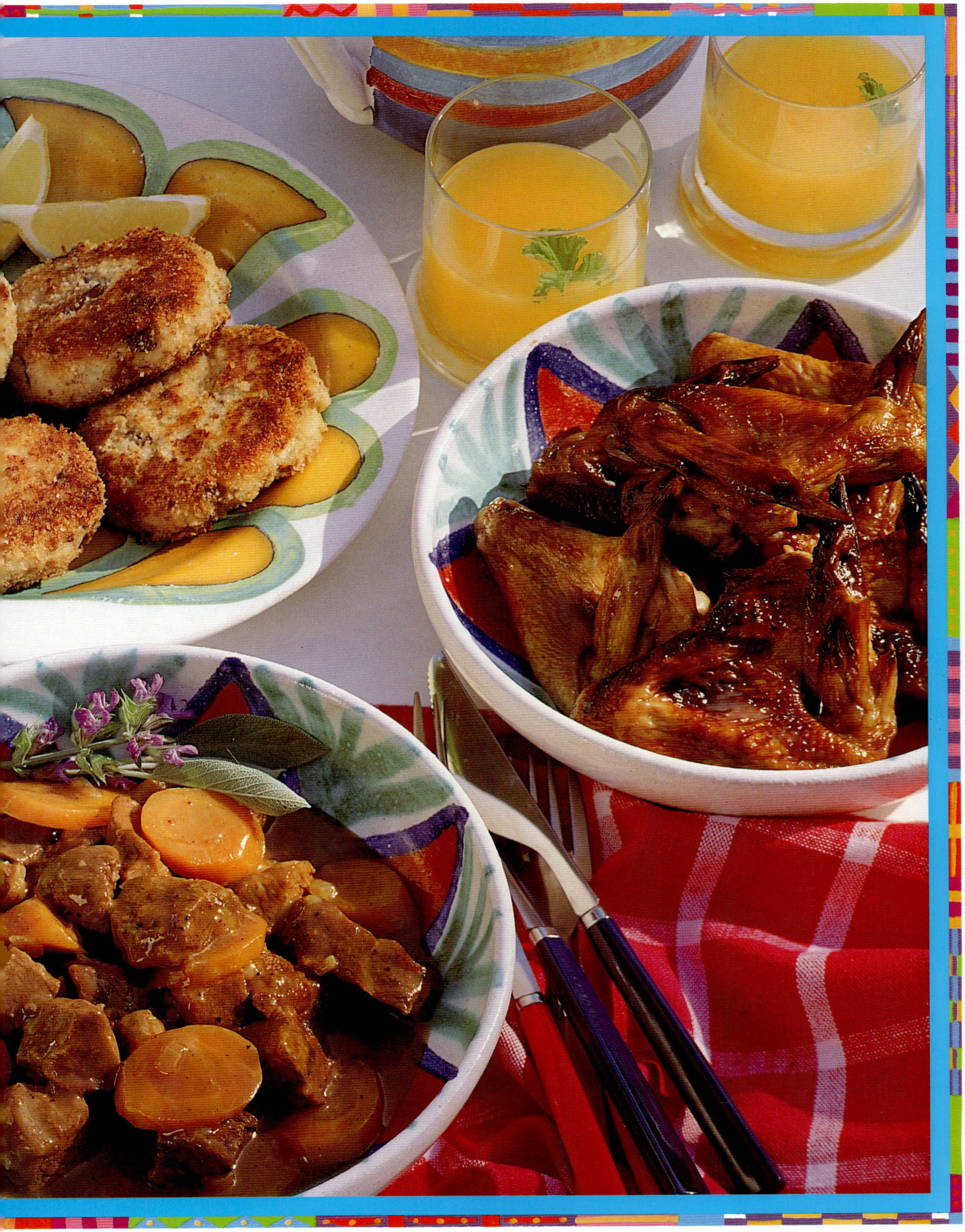

CHICKEN WINGS

Serves 4

2 tablespoons lemon juice
⅓ cup soy sauce
¼ teaspoon finely grated fresh ginger
10 chicken wings
2 tablespoons honey
2 tablespoons tomato sauce

1. Mix lemon juice, soy sauce + ginger in a large flat dish.

2. Add chicken wings, turning each till coated in sauce.

3. Cover dish and leave in fridge about 5 hours.

4. Drain the wings — save the sauce.

5. In a cup mix honey, tomato sauce + rest of soy sauce mix.

6. Grill the wings for 5 minutes. Brush them thickly with the honey mixture.

7. Grill 5 minutes more. Turn wings over, brush with more honey mixture.

8. Grill for 10 minutes more. Serve hot or cold.

CHICKEN AND GINGER

Serves 6

2 whole chicken breasts
1 teaspoon cornflour
sprinkle of salt and pepper
1 onion, finely chopped
1 stick celery, sliced
2 teaspoons finely grated fresh ginger
¼ teaspoon sugar
1 tablespoon sherry
2 tablespoons water
2 tablespoons oil
1 cup thinly sliced green beans

1.  Cut chicken meat from bones. Slice the meat thinly.
2. Put in bowl. Stir in cornflour, salt + pepper. Set it aside.
3. Put chopped onion + celery in another bowl.
4. Add ginger, sugar, sherry + water to onion + celery. Mix.
5. Heat oil in big frypan or a wok. HIGH HEAT
6. Fry chicken, stirring it until cooked. MEDIUM HEAT
7. Add onion + celery mixture. Fry it all, stirring, till cooked. MEDIUM HEAT
8. Add beans. Cook stirring till they are hot. Serve. MEDIUM HEAT

*A glutton who came from the Rhine
Was asked at what hour he would dine.
He replied, 'At eleven,
At three, five, and seven,
And eight and a quarter to nine.'*

CHICKEN AND VEGETABLES

Serves 4

- 3 chicken breast fillets
- 1 tablespoon oil
- 2 cups frozen stir-fry vegetables
- 1 tablespoon cornflour
- 1 tablespoon sherry
- ¼ cup pineapple juice
- ¼ cup water
- ½ cup drained pineapple pieces

The earliest cookbook still in existence was written by a Roman called Apicius some 2000 years ago. Apicius got his name from greedily shouting, 'I've none left, give me a piece o' yours!'

1. Chop the chicken into bite-size pieces.
2. Heat the oil in a big frypan.
3. Fry chicken, stirring, until golden + just cooked.
4. Add vegetables. Cook for 5 minutes, stirring.
5. Mix cornflour, sherry, juice and water in a cup.
6. Add, stirring until it's thickened and boiling.
7. Add pineapple. Stir it in.
8. Bring to the boil, stirring. Serve on rice.

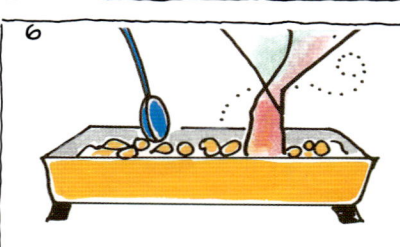

GRILLED CHICKEN

Serves 4

1 cup orange juice
2 teaspoons grated orange rind
½ teaspoon dry mustard
½ teaspoon ground nutmeg
¼ teaspoon curry powder
1 tablespoon chopped parsley
½ teaspoon instant chicken stock powder
sprinkle of salt and pepper
4 chicken breast fillets

In the days when meat was cooked over an open fire, a turnspit kept the meat turning. The turnspit was often a short-legged dog trotting round inside a wheel — the first hot dog?

1. Put orange juice, rind + mustard into a shallow dish.

2. Mix in nutmeg, curry, parsley + chicken stock. Stir well.

3. Add salt + pepper. Add chicken coating it well with juice.

4. Cover the dish with some waxed paper.

5. Put it in fridge for 2 or 3 hours, turning chicken about 2 or 3 times.

6. Take out chicken. Put it under the grill.

7. Grill it slowly, turning chicken often so it won't burn. Grill about 30 minutes.

8. Brush the rest of the marinade over chicken as it's cooking.

SALMON MORNAY

Serves 4

1½ cups cooked rice
1 x 210 g can pink salmon
1 hard-boiled egg
50 g butter
2 tablespoons plain flour
1½ cups milk
⅓ cup grated cheddar cheese
sprinkle of salt and pepper
¼ cup dry breadcrumbs

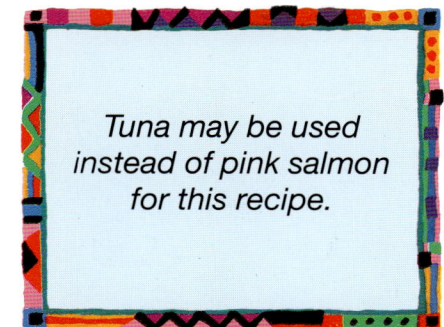

1. Turn oven to 180°C (350°F). Spread rice in baking dish.

2. Drain salmon. Remove bones. Chop up. Spread on rice.

3. Chop egg. Sprinkle over the salmon. Melt butter in a small pan.

4. Stir in flour until smooth. Take off heat. Stir in milk.

5. Reheat, stirring all the time until it boils.

6. Stir in cheese, salt and pepper. Pour it over the salmon and rice.

7. Sprinkle crumbs evenly over. Bake for 20 minutes.

Tuna may be used instead of pink salmon for this recipe.

8. Serve it hot with a tossed salad. Serves 4

TUNA LOAF

Serves 4

425 g can tuna
440 g can creamy mushroom soup
2 eggs
1½ cups cooked rice
1 small onion, finely chopped
1 celery stick, sliced
¼ cup chopped parsley
1 small grated carrot

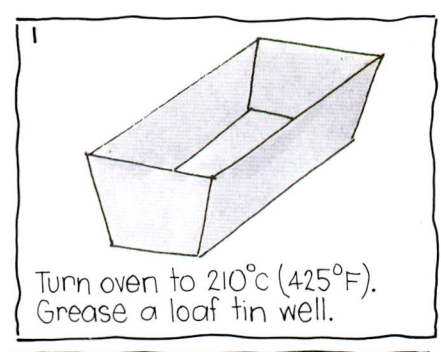

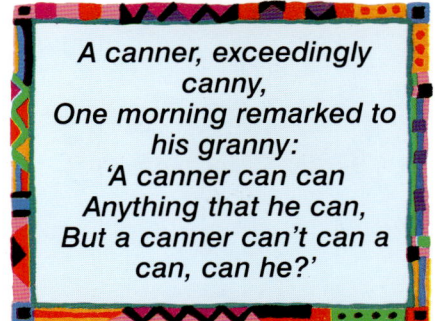

1. Turn oven to 210°C (425°F). Grease a loaf tin well.

2. Line the tin with baking paper that hangs out over the 2 long sides – YOU'LL SEE WHY LATER

3. Drain the tuna well. Flake it with a fork.

4. Put tuna in mixing bowl. Stir in the soup.

5. Add the eggs, rice, onion, celery, parsley and carrot. Mix well.

6. Spread it evenly into tin. Bake for 50 minutes.

7. Lift it out of the tin and onto a plate, using the baking paper.

A canner, exceedingly canny,
One morning remarked to his granny:
'A canner can can
Anything that he can,
But a canner can't can a can, can he?'

8. Turn out onto a plate, slice and serve with lemon wedges and a salad.

FISH CAKES

Serves 6

500 g potatoes, peeled
15 g butter
1 x 210 g can pink salmon
1 egg
salt and pepper
1 onion, peeled and finely chopped
¼ cup fresh breadcrumbs
1 cup dry packaged breadcrumbs
2 tablespoons oil

1. Boil potatoes till tender. Drain well.
2. Add butter. Mash well till smooth.
3. Drain + flake fish. Add to potatoes. Add egg, salt, pepper, onion, fresh crumbs. Mix well.
4. With lightly floured hands, shape into cakes.
5. Put dry crumbs in a dish. Coat each fish cake in crumbs.
6. Put them on a tray. Refrigerate for 1 hour.
7. Heat oil in a frypan.
8. Fry till golden on both sides. Drain and serve.

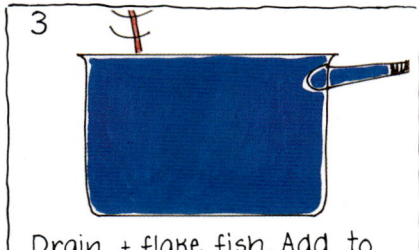

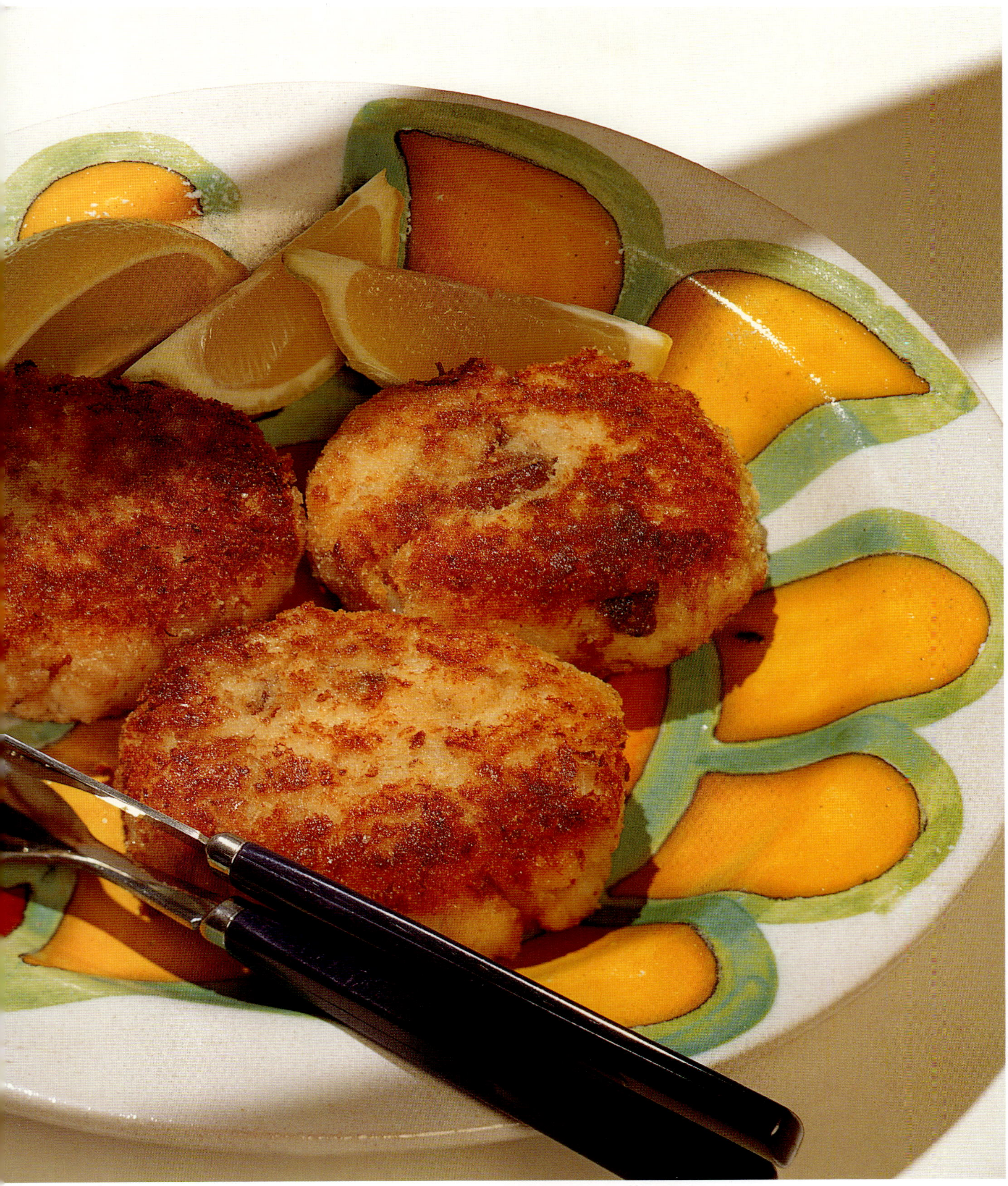

BEEF CASSEROLE

Serves 4

750 g lean stewing beef
½ cup plain flour
1 onion
1 carrot
1 beef stock cube
2 cups hot water
1 tablespoon tomato sauce
1 tablespoon Worcestershire sauce
1 tablespoon brown sugar
1 tablespoon vinegar
½ teaspoon ground nutmeg
sprinkle of salt and pepper

An easy way to coat meat in flour is to put them both into a plastic bag, seal the top and shake the bag well.

1. Turn oven to 180°C (350°F) Trim fat from the beef.
2. Slice the beef into bite-size cubes.
3. Toss beef in flour until each piece is coated.
4. Put in casserole. Peel + chop onion + carrot and add.
5. Dissolve stock cube in hot water. Stir in the sauces.
6. Stir in brown sugar, vinegar, nutmeg, salt and pepper.
7. Pour it all into casserole. Put the lid on.
8. Bake for 2 hours.

MEAT LOAF

Serves 6

1 kg lean minced beef
1 cup seasoned stuffing mix (from a packet)
1 cup tomato purée
1 egg
sprinkle of salt and pepper
2 tablespoons tomato sauce

1. Turn oven to 180°C (350°F) Put mince in a big bowl.

2. Add stuffing mix, purée, egg, salt and pepper.

3. Mix it, stirring very well until it is mixed and smooth.

4. With clean hands, shape it firmly into a loaf.

5. Put into a greased baking dish. Bake it for 1 hour.

6. Take out of oven. CAREFULLY tip away any fat.

7. Spread tomato sauce on top of loaf. Put back in oven.

8. Bake 30 minutes more. Serve hot or cold.

SWEET AND SOUR MEATBALLS

Serves 4

MEATBALLS
500 g lean minced beef
2 tablespoons plain flour
¼ teaspoon salt
2 tablespoons oil

SAUCE
1 small onion
1 green capsicum
1 tablespoon oil
1 tablespoon cornflour
1 tablespoon soy sauce
1 tablespoon brown vinegar
2 tablespoon brown sugar
1 cup pineapple pieces
½ cup pineapple juice

1. Shape mince into about 16 meatballs. Roll them in the mixed flour and salt.

2. Heat the 2 tablespoons oil. Gently fry, turning often, for about 20 minutes.

3. Meanwhile, peel + chop the onion. Slice green capsicum. Throw away the seeds.

4. Heat the 1 tablespoon oil in saucepan. Fry onion and capsicum for 3 mins.

5. Mix cornflour, soy sauce, vinegar, brown sugar, pineapple + juice in a bowl.

6. Add it all to saucepan + bring to boil, stirring it constantly. Simmer 2 mins.

7. Drain the cooked meatballs. Arrange them on a big platter of hot, cooked, rice.

Try eating Chinese-style food with the traditional chopsticks — it can be an entertaining experience and it is sure to keep the Chinese laundry in business!

8. Pour the sauce all over the meatballs. Serves 4 people.

HAM AND PINEAPPLE

Serves 4

4 canned pineapple rings in pineapple juice
2 tablespoons brown sugar
4 ham steaks (about 1 cm thick)
75 g butter

1. Drain pineapple rings. Save ½ cup of the juice.
2. Put juice + brown sugar in a large flat dish.
3. Put steaks in. Put in fridge. Leave in fridge 3 hours.
4. Turn steaks over every hour.
5. Heat butter in large frying pan. Drain the ham.
6. Fry ham till golden. Turn steaks often.
7. Fry pineapple for a few minutes at the end.
8. Serve with a salad. Serves 4 people.

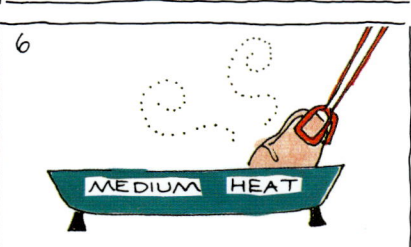

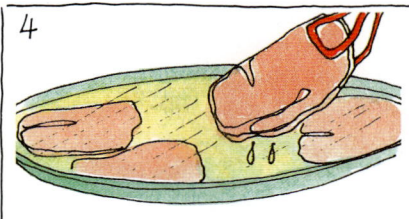

WAKE-UP BREAKFAST TRAY

Start your day off on a bright and happy note by making a special morning breakfast tray for Mum or Dad. Follow our Breakfast Checklist to make the preparation easy. Remember to collect everything you need for your recipes — all the ingredients and all the equipment.

Prepare a tray to serve your breakfast menu on. Don't forget a pretty cloth and napkin, some nice china and cutlery and perhaps a flower from the garden.

Our breakfast menu serves one person.

BREAKFAST MENU
Fruit Cup
Juice
Boiled Eggs and Toast
A pot of tea

BREAKFAST CHECKLIST

1. Collect all the things you will need for the tray:
   - a placemat and napkin
   - small bowl for Fruit Cup
   - glass for Juice
   - serving plate and egg cup for Eggs and Toast
   - cup, saucer and spoon
   - perhaps a flower, the morning paper or magazine.
2. Make the Fruit Cup.
3. Put the water for the eggs on to boil.
4. Squeeze the Fresh Juice.
5. Add the eggs to the boiling water.
6. Put the kettle on.
7. Warm the teapot.
8. Make the pot of tea (add milk and sugar to the cup if needed).
9. Make the toast, remove the eggs and place on serving plate.
10. Place the Fruit Cup, Juice, Eggs and Toast and pot of tea on the breakfast tray and serve.

FRUIT CUP

Choose any fresh or canned fruits. Try fresh strawberries and apple or peaches or pears. Use canned mandarin segments and fresh grapes or canned pineapple with chopped mint.

**1 cup chopped fruit
1 tablespoon orange juice
½ teaspoon sugar
2 tablespoons plain yoghurt**

1. Place your choice of fruit in a small serving bowl.
2. Pour over the orange juice and sprinkle with sugar.
3. Spoon the yoghurt on top of fruit.

FRESH JUICE

Nothing is nicer than freshly squeezed juice for breakfast. Use fresh oranges or grapefruit or a mixture of both.

2 or 3 oranges

1. Cut oranges in half and use a juicer, twisting left and right to extract all the juice.
2. Carefully pour the juice into a tall glass, taking care not to pour in the seeds. Add a few ice cubes if you like to make the juice really cold.

BOILED EGGS AND TOAST

water
1 or 2 eggs
2 slices of bread
butter

1. Fill a small saucepan with water, place on the stove and turn the heat to high.
2. When the water boils use a spoon to carefully lower each egg into the water. For a soft-boiled egg (white just set, yolk runny) boil for 4 minutes; for a medium-boiled egg (hard white, half-solid yolk) boil for 6 minutes; for a hard-boiled egg (hard white, hard yolk) boil for 11 minutes.
3. Towards the end of the egg cooking time, toast the bread and spread with butter or margarine.
4. When the eggs are ready carefully remove from the water with a slotted spoon. Place the eggs in egg cups and use a spoon to lightly crack the top of the egg. Serve with the hot buttered toast.

A POT OF TEA

boiling water
loose tea or tea bags
milk
sugar

1. Put a kettle of fresh water on to boil and when it boils carefully pour a little water into the teapot (this warms the pot). Let this stand for a few minutes.
2. Throw away the water in the teapot and boil the kettle again. Add 2 heaped teaspoons of tea to the pot (one for each person and one for the pot) and pour in the boiling water. Put the lid on the pot and stand for 2 minutes before serving.

1 Pour a little hot water into the pot to warm it. Empty before adding tea.

1 Cut oranges in half and use a juicer to squeeze out juice.

1 Use a spoon to lower eggs into boiling water.

2 Add tea to pot: 1 heaped teaspoon for each person and 1 for the pot.

2 Carefully pour the juice into a glass. Take care not to add seeds.

2 Crack the egg with a small spoon to remove the top.

3 Carefully pour in boiling water. Stand for 2 minutes before pouring.

CHAPTER FOUR
PIES, PASTA AND PIZZA

Perfect pies, pasta and pizza — all these family favourites satisfy hungry appetites. They are fast and easy to make and will be eaten up quickly, too.

53

ONION TART

Serves 6

375 g puff pastry
¾ cup grated cheese
50 g butter
2 onions, finely sliced
1 cup evaporated milk
1 tablespoon plain flour
sprinkle of salt and pepper
2 eggs

1. Turn oven to 190°C (375°F). Roll out the pastry.
2. Line a 24 cm pie dish. Trim edges neatly.
3. Sprinkle cheese over base. Put it in the fridge until the filling is ready.
4. Melt butter in pan. Gently cook onion until soft but not brown.
5. Whisk milk, flour, salt, pepper, eggs in a bowl.
6. Stir in the onions and the butter.
7. Carefully pour it all into the pastry base.
8. Bake 35-40 minutes or until it is set.

SAVOURY PIE

Serves 4

1 small onion
1 x 500 g can minced beef
½ cup uncooked rice
1 cup tomato purée
sprinkle of salt and pepper
3 slices bread
30 g butter

1. Chop the onion finely. Put in a big saucepan.
2. Add mince, rice, tomato purée, salt and pepper.
3. Mix it all together very well.
4. Bring it to the boil, stirring it all the time. (MEDIUM HEAT)
5. Simmer gently for 30 minutes stirring now and then. (LOW HEAT)
6. Spread evenly in big pie dish or flat casserole.
7. Butter bread. Cut into tiny cubes. Sprinkle on top.
8. Bake it at 180°C (350°F) for 15 minutes, then put it under grill and grill for 5 minutes or till top is crisp.

SAUSAGE PIE

Serves 6

6 sausages
boiling water
375 g puff pastry
4 eggs
sprinkle of salt and pepper

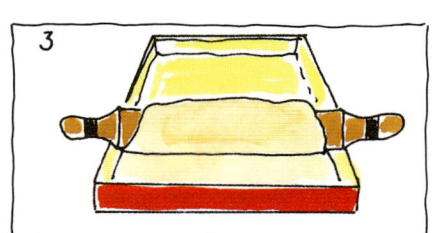

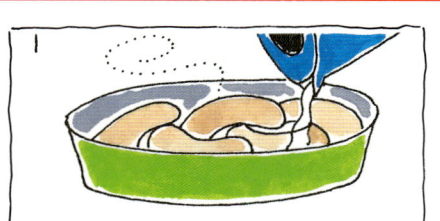

1. Put sausages in a pan. Pour boiling water over. Leave until cool.

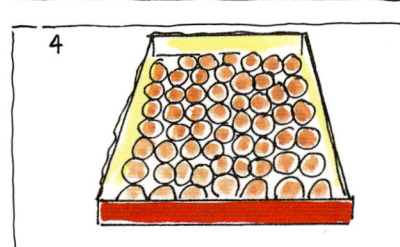

2. When cool, carefully peel the skin from the sausages.

3. Cut pastry in half. Roll half out and line a 25 cm square tin with it.

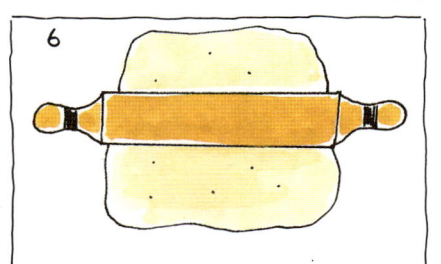

4. Slice up sausages. Arrange evenly in the tin.

5. Beat eggs, salt + pepper. Gently pour over sausages.

6. Roll out rest of pastry to make a lid. Place over sausages.

7. Seal the edges well. Prick top with a fork.

8. Bake it at 190°C (375°F) for 45 minutes. Serve hot or cold.

MACARONI BAKE

Serves 4

- 1½ cups small macaroni
- 1 big pan of boiling water
- 4 rashers of bacon
- 1 onion, peeled and chopped
- 1 x 440 g can tomato soup
- ½ cup milk
- 1 cup grated cheese

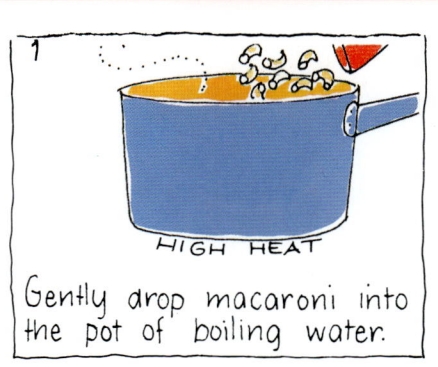

1. Gently drop macaroni into the pot of boiling water. (HIGH HEAT)
2. Keep it boiling well for 8 minutes. (HIGH HEAT)
3. Drain well. Put it into an 8-cup casserole.
4. Chop bacon. Fry gently with onion till cooked. (MEDIUM HEAT)
5. Drain it. Stir it into the casserole.
6. Stir in soup, milk and the grated cheese.
7. Bake it at 190°C (375°F) for 45 minutes.
8. Serve HOT with a tossed salad and French bread. Serves 4-5.

MACARONI MINCE

Serves 4

1 tablespoon oil
1 onion, finely chopped
500 g lean minced beef
sprinkle of salt and pepper
425 g can peeled tomatoes
¾ cup tomato purée
1 teaspoon dried oregano
¼ teaspoon sugar
1 cup water
1½ cups small shell macaroni

Some pasta names have interesting meanings: fettuccine — ribbons, farfalle — butterflies, penne — quills or pens, while vermicelli means little worms.

1. Heat oil in a big pan. Fry onion until soft.
2. Add mince. Cook, stirring till all red has gone.
3. Add salt, pepper, canned tomatoes, purée, oregano, sugar and water.
4. Stir it all together well until it starts to boil.
5. Turn heat to low and simmer for 40 minutes.
6. Drop macaroni into a big pot of boiling water.
7. Boil macaroni 10 minutes. Drain it well.
8. Put in a casserole. Pour hot mince over + serve.

BIG PIZZA

Serves 4

- 2 cups self-raising flour
- ¼ teaspoon salt
- 30 g butter
- 1 cup milk
- 1 tablespoon oil
- ¼ cup tomato sauce
- 2 cups grated Cheddar cheese
- 1 tomato, thinly sliced
- 1 cup well drained pineapple pieces
- 1 cup finely chopped ham (or salami)

> Patient: Doctor, I have a piece of bacon growing out of my ear.
> Doctor: Don't worry, I'll soon cure it.

1. Turn oven to 220°C (425°F). Get out a large oven tray.
2. Sift flour + salt into bowl. Chop up butter and add.
3. Use your fingertips to rub together the flour and butter until they look like breadcrumbs.
4. Add milk (more if needed) and knead + mix to a soft dough.
5. Roll it out on the baking tray until 34 cm in diameter.
6. Brush dough with oil then the tomato sauce.
7. Sprinkle cheese over, arrange tomato slices on top.
8. Spread pineapple and ham evenly over. Bake 20-25 minutes or until cooked.

CHAPTER FIVE
Microwave Cookery

Microwave magic gives you main dishes, soup, snacks and desserts in record time. Make the most of microwaving with Ham and Cheese Bread or Pavlova Roll.

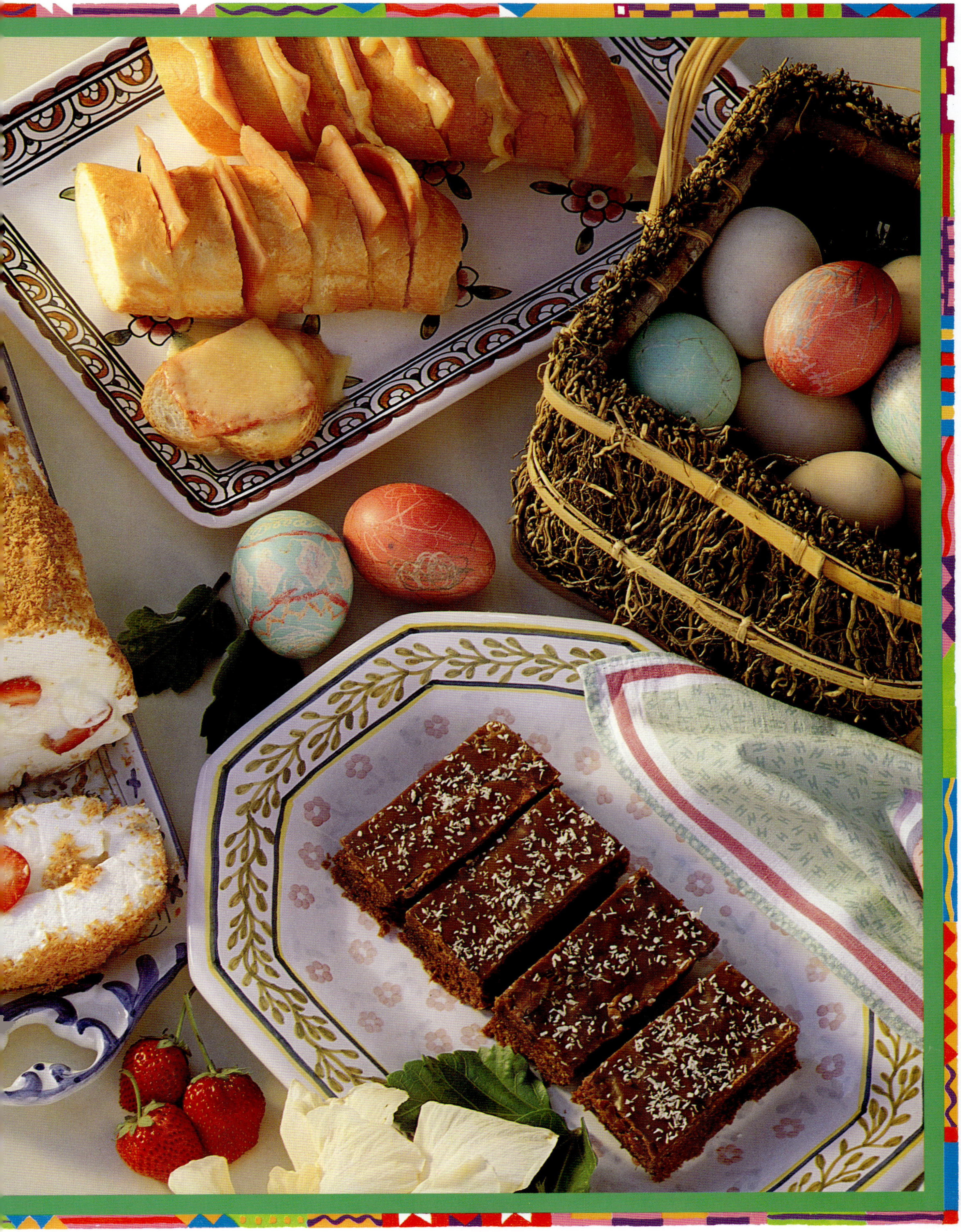

CHICKEN AND CORN SOUP

Serves 6

3 teaspoons chicken stock powder
3½ cups boiling water
1 cup chopped cooked chicken
1 cup canned cream-style sweet corn

2 teaspoons cornflour
a little cold water
1 tablespoon chopped parsley
sprinkle of pepper

> Beautiful Soup! Who cares for fish, game or any other dish? Who would not give all else for two pennyworth only of beautiful soup! Beau-ootiful Soo-oop!

1. Put stock powder + boiling water in a big bowl.
2. Add chicken + canned corn. Stir well.
3. Cover with a paper towel.
4. Microwave on High for 6 - 6½ minutes until boiling - stirring once.
5. Mix cornflour + cold water in a cup until smooth.
6. Stir in to soup. Stir well. Cover with paper towel.
7. Bring to boil - microwave on High for 1½ - 2 minutes.
8. Stir in parsley and pepper. Serve.

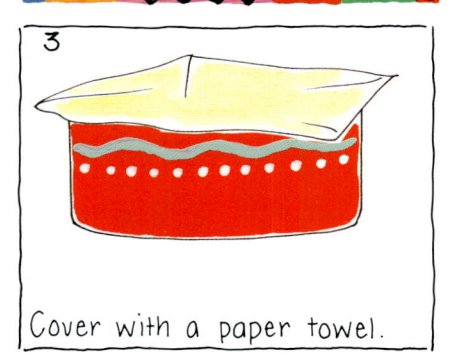

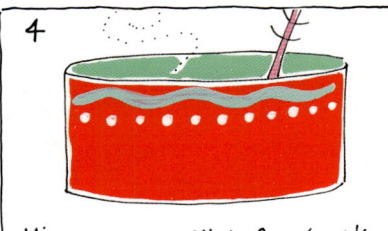

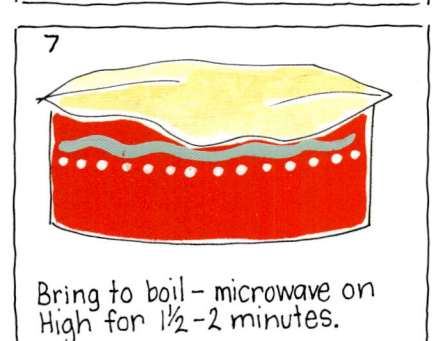

CHEESE SNACK

Serves 1

1 slice of bread
2 teaspoons tomato sauce or chutney
cheese

1. Toast the bread.
2. Spread with tomato sauce.
3. Slice cheese thinly.
4. Cover sauce with cheese.
5. Put on a plate.
6. Cook on High for 18-20 seconds.
7. Watch it - take out when cheese melts.
8. Serve.

HAM AND CHEESE BREAD

Serves 6

1 French stick (about 25 cm long)

8–10 slices cheese, thinly sliced

8–10 slices ham

1 Slice French bread (not quite through) 8 or 10 times.

2 Trim cheese to about the size of diameter of bread.

3 Trim ham to about the same size.

4 Place ham + cheese together in each cut.

5 Put on a paper towel.

6 Cook on High 1–2 minutes.

7 Watch for cheese to start melting, then take out.

8 Serve cut through.

CREAMY CHICKEN

Serves 4

4 chicken breast fillets
½ teaspoon sweet paprika
1 onion, peeled and chopped
1 apple, peeled and chopped
1 x 440 g can cream of mushroom soup
½ teaspoon curry powder
¾ cup milk

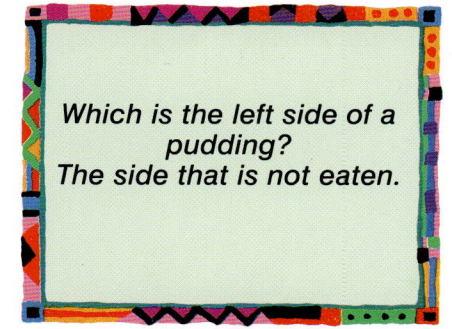

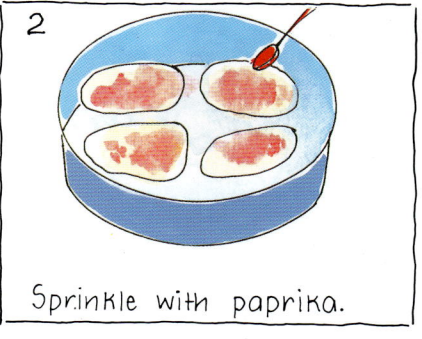

*Which is the left side of a pudding?
The side that is not eaten.*

1. Take skin off chicken. Put in one layer in a dish.
2. Sprinkle with paprika.
3. Sprinkle chopped onion + apple over.
4. Mix soup, curry, milk well in a jug.
5. Pour over chicken. Cover with cling wrap. Prick.
6. Cook on Medium (70%) for 15 minutes.
7. Take out. Spoon the sauce over.
8. Cover again. Cook on Medium (70%) for 8-10 minutes.

SPANISH OMELETTE

Serves 4

1 small onion, finely chopped
15 g butter
1 cooked potato, chopped
1 tomato, chopped
1 small green capsicum, finely chopped
sprinkle of salt and pepper
3 eggs
2 tablespoons milk

1. Put chopped onion + butter in a bowl.
2. Cover with cling wrap. Prick. Microwave on High for 2 minutes.
3. Add potato, tomato, capsicum, salt + pepper.
4. Add eggs + milk. Stir it all well.
5. Pour into a greased 20 cm pie plate.
6. Cover with cling wrap. Prick. Microwave on High for 1½ minutes.
7. Stir cooked egg to centre. Cover. Cook on High 1¾ minutes.
8. Stir again. Cook (uncovered) 1 minute. Stand 2 mins. Serve.

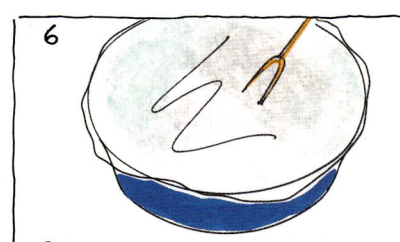

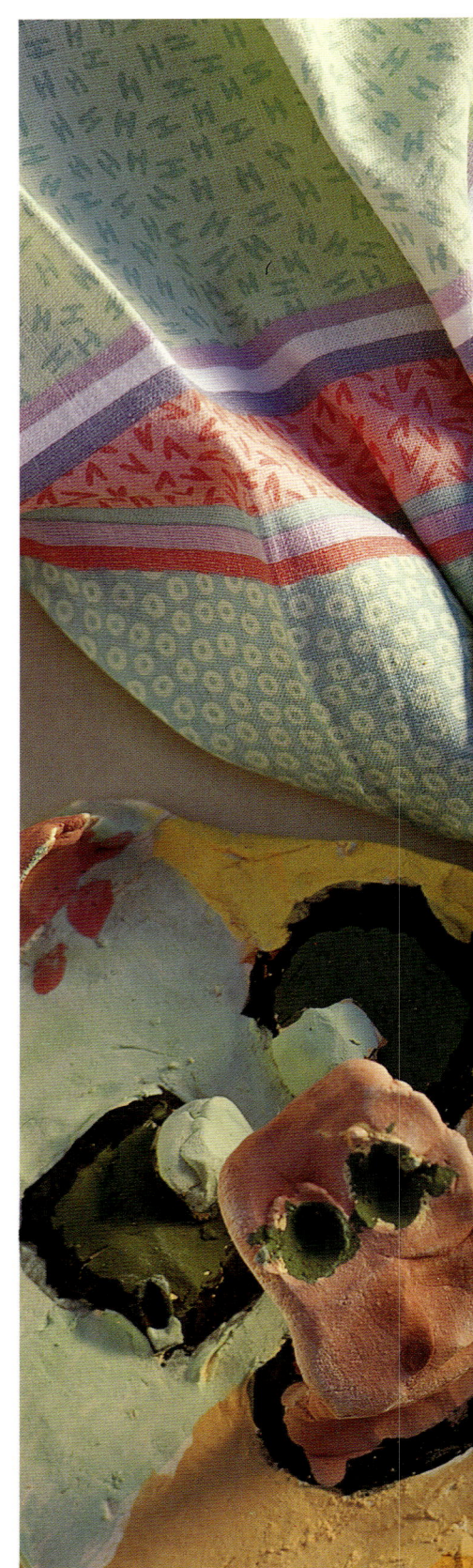

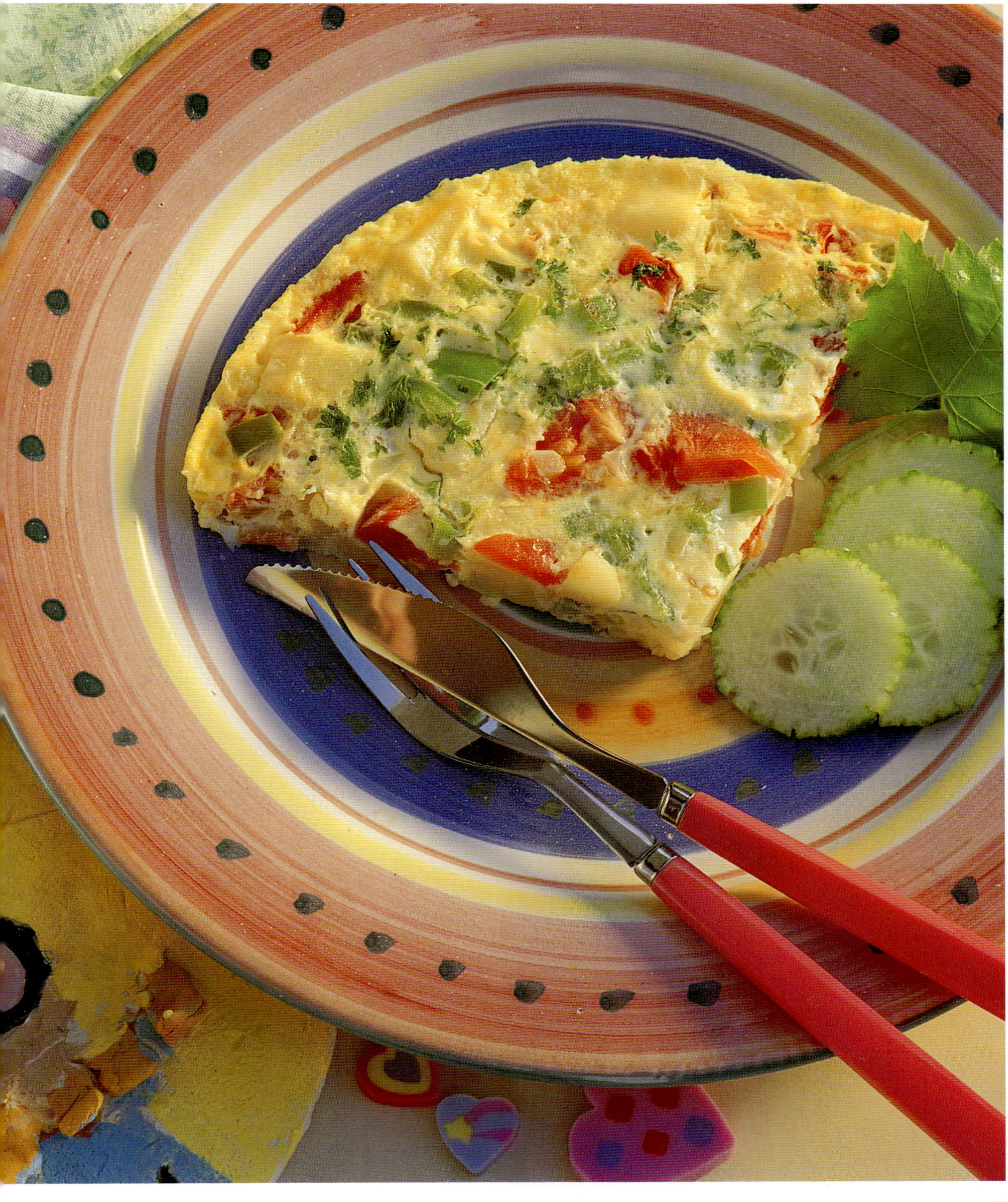

CHEESE AND POTATO BAKE

Serves 6

30 g butter
1 onion, peeled and chopped
6 medium-sized potatoes
sprinkle of salt and pepper
⅔ cup milk
¾ cup grated Cheddar cheese

1. Put butter + onion in a bowl. Cook on High 3 minutes.

2. Peel the potatoes. Slice them up thinly.

3. Put half the potatoes into a 22cm round casserole.

4. Spread onion + butter over. Sprinkle with salt + pepper.

5. Arrange rest of potatoes evenly over.

6. Pour the milk over. Sprinkle cheese on top.

7. Cover with cling wrap. Prick. Microwave on High for 8 minutes.

8. Remove cover. Microwave on High for 10 minutes or until tender. If you like, put under grill to brown cheese and serve.

PAVLOVA ROLL

Serves 6

butter and cornflour to grease and dust tray
4 egg whites (at room temperature)
1 cup caster sugar
¾ teaspoon imitation vanilla essence
1 teaspoon white vinegar
½ cup toasted coconut, and more for Step 6
300 mL cream, whipped
1 cup sliced fruit, e.g. strawberries or banana

Did you know that there are only six things that you need to eat in order to be healthy? They are: carbohydrates, proteins, fats, water, minerals and vitamins. So why are you so spotty?

1. Grease lightly a 24×24cm micro dish. Line with paper.
2. Grease paper. Sprinkle with cornflour. Shake off excess.
3. Beat egg whites until stiff.
4. Add sugar very slowly, beating all the time. Blend in vanilla + vinegar.
5. Spread evenly on tray. Sprinkle with coconut. Microwave on High for 2 minutes. Cool.
6. Sprinkle a sheet of waxed paper with more coconut. Turn cold pavlova onto it.
7. Spread with whipped cream and fruit.
8. Carefully roll up. Slide onto serving plate.

PINEAPPLE CAKE

Makes 1 x 20 cm cake
- 60 g butter
- ¾ cup caster sugar
- 1 teaspoon imitation vanilla essence
- 1 egg
- ½ cup milk
- 1 cup crushed pineapple
- ½ cup coconut
- 1½ cups self-raising flour

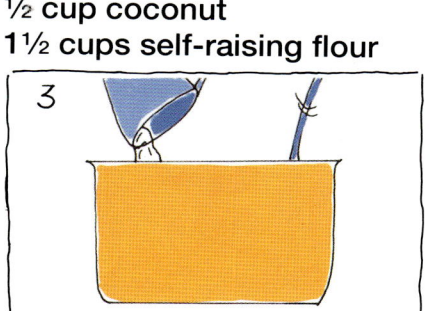

1. Cream butter, sugar until smooth.
2. Add vanilla and egg. Beat well.
3. Add milk, drained pineapple, coconut. Stir well.
4. Sift in self-raising flour. Mix well.
5. Pour into greased 20 cm ring mould - 7 cm deep.
6. Microwave on rack for 7½-8 minutes on Medium (70%) uncovered.
7. Microwave on High for 4-4½ minutes more.
8. Stand 5 minutes. Tip out. Ice when cool. (See page 88)

CHOCOLATE CRUNCH

Makes about 16 slices

180 g butter
1 cup cornflakes
1 cup desiccated coconut
¾ cup caster sugar
1 cup self-raising flour
2 tablespoons cocoa

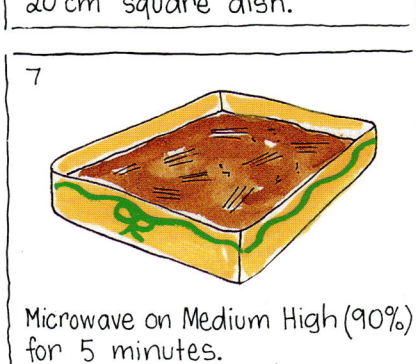

1. Put butter in small bowl. Cover with paper towel.
2. Microwave it on Medium (50%) for 2½ minutes, until it melts.
3. Put cornflakes, coconut, sugar in a bowl.
4. Sift in flour + cocoa.
5. Add melted butter. Mix well.
6. Press firmly into greased 20 cm square dish.
7. Microwave on Medium High (90%) for 5 minutes.
8. Ice with chocolate icing (See page 91) while still warm.

CHAPTER SIX
DESSERTS

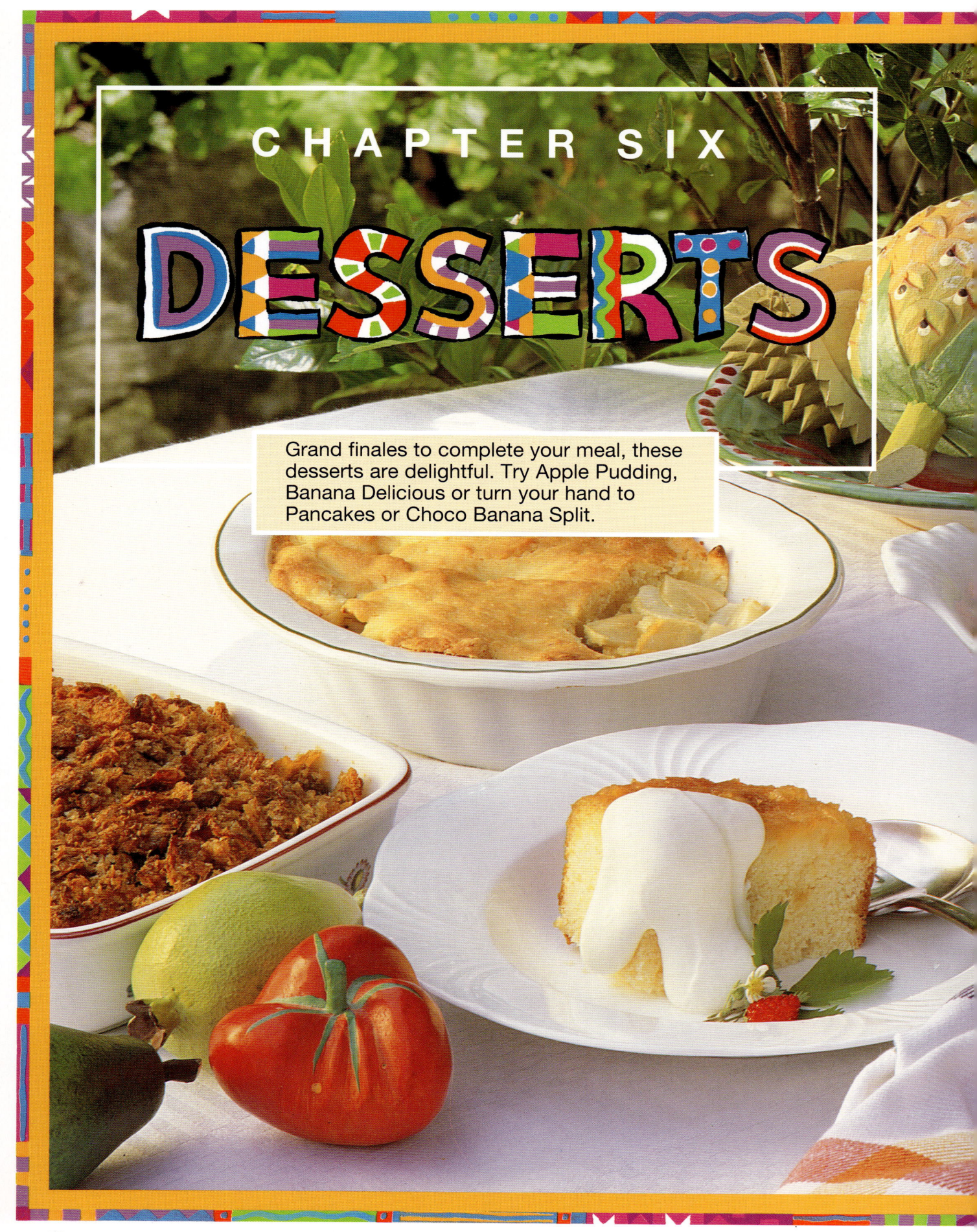

Grand finales to complete your meal, these desserts are delightful. Try Apple Pudding, Banana Delicious or turn your hand to Pancakes or Choco Banana Split.

73

APPLE PUDDING

Serves 6

5 green apples
¼ cup caster sugar
1 teaspoon grated lemon rind
1 tablespoon water
60 g butter
2 tablespoons caster sugar, extra
1 egg
½ cup self-raising flour
cream or ice-cream, to serve

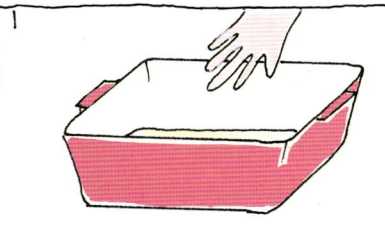

1. Turn oven to 180°C (350°F). Grease a baking dish.

2. Peel, core + slice apples. Put in baking dish.

3. Stir in caster sugar + lemon rind. Add the water.

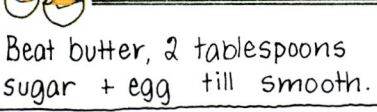

4. Beat butter, 2 tablespoons sugar + egg till smooth.

5. Stir in the flour. Mix well.

6. Carefully spread it on top of the apples.

7. Bake it for 30-35 minutes or until golden.

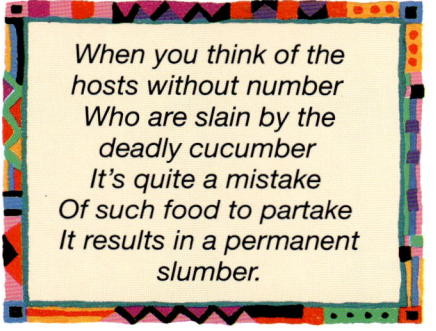

*When you think of the hosts without number
Who are slain by the deadly cucumber
It's quite a mistake
Of such food to partake
It results in a permanent slumber.*

8. Serve warm with cream or vanilla ice-cream.

BAKED APPLES

Serves 4

4 green apples
½ cup finely chopped dates
1 tablespoon chopped walnuts
1 tablespoon grated lemon rind
½ cup water
½ cup brown sugar
30 g butter
¼ teaspoon ground cinnamon
¼ teaspoon ground nutmeg
ice-cream or whipped cream, to serve

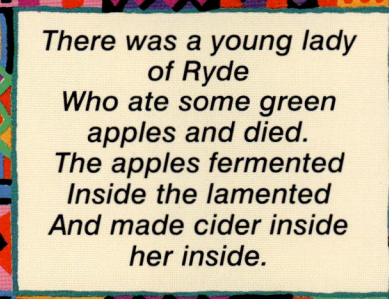

1. Turn oven to 180°C (350°F) Cut core neatly out of apples.
2. Peel the top quarter off each apple.
3. Mix dates, walnuts + rind well. Press into centres of apples.
4. Put apples into a pan or a loaf tin.
5. Put water, brown sugar, butter, cinnamon + nutmeg in a pan.
6. Bring it to the boil and pour it over the apples.
7. Bake them for about 1¼ hours - basting now + again with the liquid.
8. Serve apples hot with vanilla ice-cream or whipped cream.

> There was a young lady of Ryde
> Who ate some green apples and died.
> The apples fermented
> Inside the lamented
> And made cider inside her inside.

UPSIDE-DOWN CAKE

Serves 6

- 125 g butter
- ¾ cup caster sugar
- 1 egg
- 2 cups plain flour
- 2 teaspoons baking powder
- ¾ cup milk
- 1 large banana, mashed
- 75 g butter, melted
- ½ cup brown sugar
- 1 cup well drained crushed pineapple
- cream, to serve

> 'I must leave here,' said Lady de Vere,
> 'For these damp airs don't suit me, I fear.'
> Said a lady, 'Dear me! If they do not agree
> With your system, why eat pears, my dear?

1. Turn oven to 180°C (350°F). Have ready a 20 cm square tin.
2. Beat butter, sugar, egg till smooth. Sift in flour + baking powder.
3. Mix it in adding milk and mashed banana as well.
4. Spread melted butter in base of the tin.
5. Sprinkle brown sugar evenly in the base.
6. Carefully spread crushed pineapple over.
7. Pour batter evenly over. Bake for 1 hour.
8. Tip out onto plate. Serve warm with cream.

BANANA DELICIOUS

Serves 6

4 medium-sized bananas
1 tablespoon lemon juice
2 eggs
2 tablespoons caster sugar
1 cup desiccated coconut
2 tablespoons apricot jam
cream or ice-cream to serve

1. Turn oven to 180°C (350°F). Peel the bananas.
2. Slice the bananas into an ovenproof dish.
3. Sprinkle the lemon juice all over.
4. Put eggs + sugar in bowl. Beat well until creamy.
5. Stir in coconut + jam. Mix it all well.
6. Pour it all evenly over the bananas.
7. Bake for 25 minutes or until golden.
8. Serve warm with cream or ice-cream.

PANCAKES

Makes about 12

1 cup plain flour
sprinkle of salt
1 egg
1¼ cups milk
a little oil to grease frypan
lemon juice } to sprinkle
sugar   } over pancakes
cream or ice-cream, to serve

1. Sift flour + salt into mixing bowl. Add egg and milk.

2. Whisk + whisk till smooth. NO LUMPS! Set aside for 1 hour.

3. Gently heat a lightly greased 20 cm frypan. MEDIUM HEAT

4. Pour batter into a jug for easier pouring.

5. Pour about 3 tablespoons into pan. Tilt pan to spread it all over evenly.

6. Lift edges with a knife. When golden, flip it over and cook the other side.

7. Place on kitchen paper. Sprinkle lemon + sugar over.

8. Roll up and serve hot with whipped cream or ice-cream if you like.

FRUIT CRUMBLE

Serves 6

1 cup canned peach slices
1 cup pineapple pieces
50 g butter
½ cup brown sugar
1 cup bran
1 cup cornflakes
cream or ice-cream, to serve

1. Turn oven to 180°C. Drain peaches + pineapples.
2. Put the fruit into an ovenproof dish.
3. Put butter in a pan. Melt on low heat.
4. Take off heat. Stir in brown sugar.
5. Add bran + cornflakes. Stir it well.
6. Sprinkle it evenly over the fruit.
7. Bake for 12-15 minutes.
8. Serve warm with cream or ice-cream.

STEAMED PUDDING

Serves 6

½ cup strawberry jam
60 g butter
½ cup caster sugar
1 egg

1½ cups plain flour
1 teaspoon baking powder
½ cup milk

1. Grease a 4 cup pudding bowl. Spread jam in the base.
2. Beat butter, sugar + egg till smooth and creamy. 
3. Sift in flour + baking powder. Add milk and mix well. 
4. Spread it carefully on top of the jam in bowl. 
5. Make a foil lid. Press the edges to seal tight. Make a string handle for it.  
6. Lower it into big pan with boiling water 5cm deep in it. HIGH HEAT
7. Put lid on pan. Turn heat to low. Simmer for 1¼ hours. Keep refilling with water. LOW HEAT
8. Run knife round edge of pudding. Tip onto serving plate. Serve.

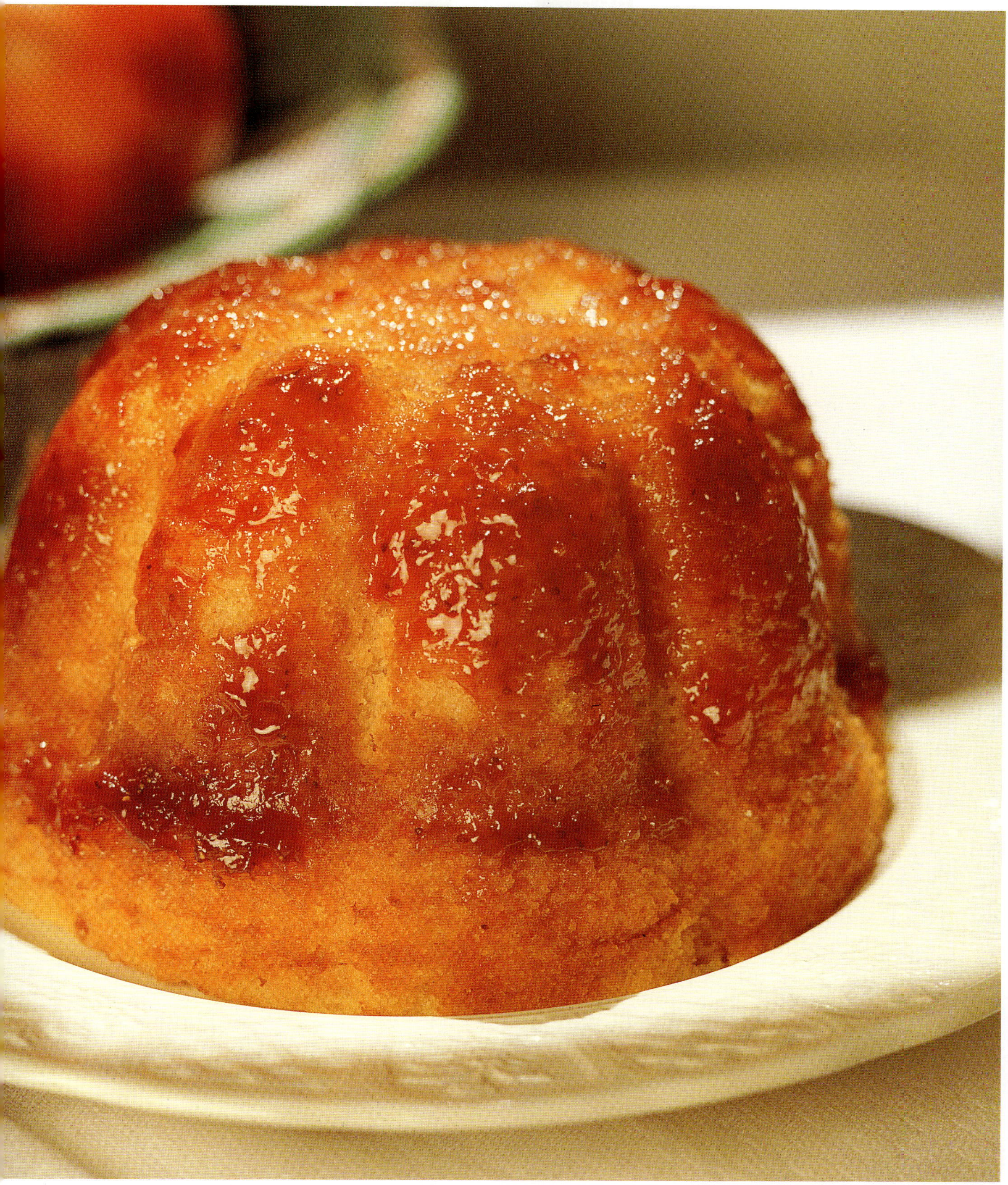

CHOCOLATE SUNDAE

Serves 4

1 teaspoon cornflour
2 tablespoons cocoa
25 g butter
⅓ cup golden syrup
¼ cup water
4 scoops vanilla ice-cream
chopped walnuts (if liked)

1. Mix cornflour + cocoa powder in a small pan.
2. Add the butter and the golden syrup.
3. Add the water.
4. Melt it all together. LOW HEAT
5. Stir well, simmering gently. LOW HEAT
6. Put a scoop of ice-cream into 4 nice dishes.
7. Pour some of the hot sauce over each one.
8. Scatter a few walnuts on top if you like.

CHOCO BANANA SPLIT

Serves 4

¾ cup caster sugar
3 tablespoons cocoa
2 tablespoons water
¾ cup evaporated milk
2 tablespoons butter
½ teaspoon imitation vanilla essence
4 medium-sized bananas
4 scoops vanilla ice-cream

1. Put sugar, cocoa, and water in a small pan.
2. Add milk. Stir it until it comes to the boil.
3. Simmer gently for 5 minutes. Stir in butter and vanilla.
4. Set it aside to cool for about 10 minutes.
5. Peel, then split the bananas in half.
6. Put 2 halves in each of 4 nice sundae dishes.
7. Put a scoop of ice-cream on top of each.
8. Pour chocolate sauce over each and serve.

APPLE TURNOVERS

Serves 6

about 200 g puff pastry
2 green apples
2 tablespoons caster sugar
2 teaspoons ground cinnamon

1. Turn oven to 190°C (375°F) Roll pastry out thinly.

2. Cut into 6 squares 14 × 14 cm

3. Peel + core apples. Cut into quarters. Slice very thinly.

4. Put a few slices of apple in corner of pastry.

5. Sprinkle apple with a teaspoon sugar. Add a pinch of cinnamon.

6. Fold over into neat triangles. Press edges with fork to seal well.

7. Prick a hole in top. Sprinkle a little sugar over.

8. Place on a baking tray. Bake 20 minutes.

FRUIT FLUMMERY

Serves 6

½ cup cold water
1 tablespoon gelatine
¼ cup plain flour
¾ cup caster sugar
½ cup apple juice
1 teaspoon lemon juice
1 cup hot water
the pulp of 4 passionfruit
plain yoghurt, to serve

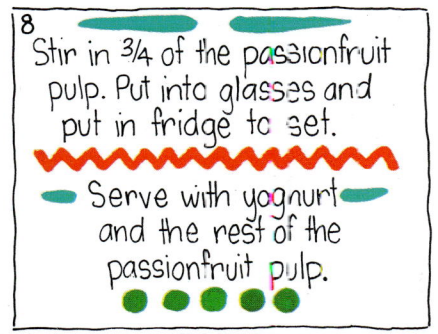

1. Whisk cold water + gelatine. Set aside.
2. Put flour + sugar in small pan. Add apple juice. Whisk.
3. Add lemon juice + hot water. Whisk.
4. Stir over heat until it's thick and bubbly. MEDIUM HEAT
5. Take off heat. Add the gelatine. Whisk well.
6. Pour into a bowl. Chill in fridge till it thickens. DON'T let it set!
7. Beat it hard (about 5 minutes) until very thick and pale.
8. Stir in ¾ of the passionfruit pulp. Put into glasses and put in fridge to set. Serve with yoghurt and the rest of the passionfruit pulp.

CHAPTER SEVEN
CAKES

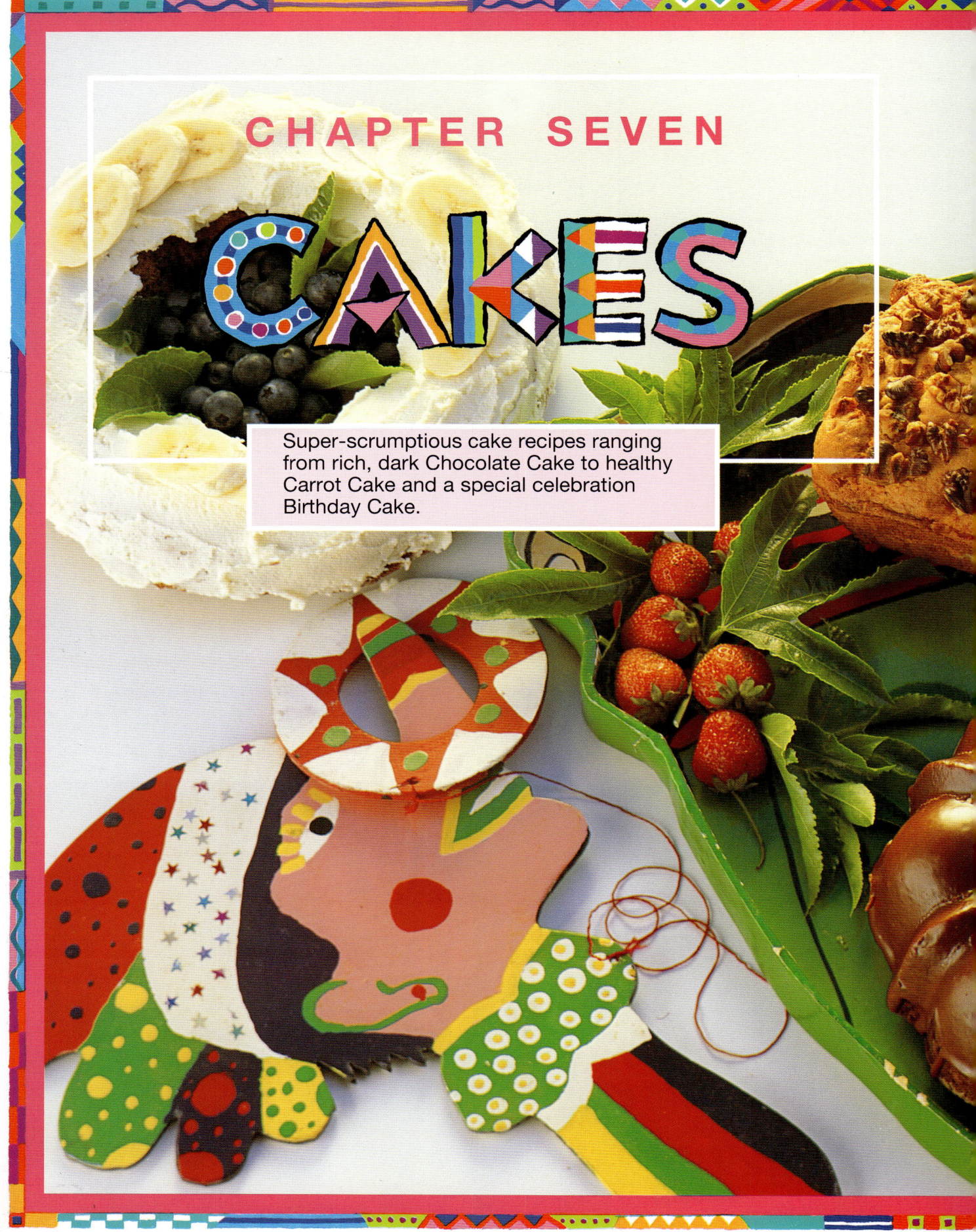

Super-scrumptious cake recipes ranging from rich, dark Chocolate Cake to healthy Carrot Cake and a special celebration Birthday Cake.

87

CARROT CAKE

Makes 1 x 20 cm cake

- 1½ cups raw sugar
- 1 cup oil
- 4 eggs
- 3 cups grated carrot
- 2 cups wholemeal self-raising flour
- 1 teaspoon ground cinnamon

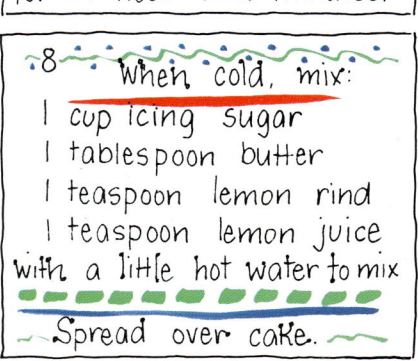

1. Turn oven to 180°C (350°F). Grease a 20 cm tin and line base with waxed paper.
2. Put raw sugar + oil in a mixing bowl. Beat well.
3. Add eggs and beat well.
4. Put grated carrot into a large mixing bowl.
5. Sift in wholemeal flour and cinnamon.
6. Pour the egg mixture in. Mix it all well.
7. Pour into tin and bake for 1 hour + 10 minutes.
8. When cold, mix:
   - 1 cup icing sugar
   - 1 tablespoon butter
   - 1 teaspoon lemon rind
   - 1 teaspoon lemon juice

   with a little hot water to mix. Spread over cake.

CHOCOLATE CAKE

Makes 1 x 20 cm cake
125 g butter
¾ cup caster sugar
2 eggs
1 tablespoon golden syrup
1 teaspoon imitation vanilla essence
1 cup milk
1½ cups self-raising flour
2 tablespoons cocoa

1. Turn oven to 180°C (350°F) Grease a 20cm star-shaped or round tin.
2. Line base of tin with greased waxed paper.
3. Beat butter, sugar + eggs till smooth + creamy.
4. Stir in golden syrup and vanilla.
5. Mix in milk
6. Sift in flour and cocoa. Mix in well.
7. Spread evenly in tin. Bake 45-55 minutes.
8. After 10 minutes take out of tin. Cool completely. Ice with chocolate icing from Fudge Cake, page 91.

BANANA CAKE

Makes 1 x 20 cm cake
60 g butter
½ cup caster sugar
1 egg
1 teaspoon imitation vanilla essence
1 cup self-raising flour
¼ cup milk
1 ripe banana, mashed
icing, see page 88

1. Turn oven to 180°C (350°F). Grease well a 20cm ring tin.

2. Dust all over the inside of tin with a little flour.

3. Gently melt butter in a big pan. Don't let it boil.

4. Take off heat and add sugar, egg + vanilla.

5. Beat it well with a wooden spoon until smooth.

6. Sift in flour. Don't stir it yet!

7. Add milk + mashed banana. Stir until just mixed.

8. Spread evenly in tin. Bake for 30 minutes. Ice cake when cold.

FUDGE CAKE

Makes 1 x 20 cm cake
1½ cups self-raising flour
3 tablespoons cocoa
1 cup caster sugar
1 cup water
1 teaspoon imitation vanilla essence
1 tablespoon white vinegar
½ cup vegetable oil

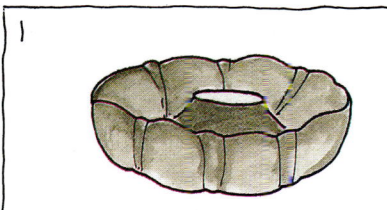

1 Turn oven to 180°C (350°F) Grease a 20cm fluted ring tin.

2 Dust the inside of the tin with a little flour.

3 Put 1½ cups flour, cocoa, sugar + water in a bowl.

4 Add vanilla, vinegar and oil.

5 Mix it all together with a whisk.

6 When smooth, pour it into the tin.

7 Bake 35-40 minutes. Cool for 10 minutes then take out of tin.

8 ICING
Mix: 1 cup icing sugar
1½ tablespoons cocoa
1 tablespoon butter
with a little hot water.
(Use more water if you want the icing runny.)
Ice the cake.

APRICOT LOAF

Makes 1 loaf

½ cup finely chopped dried apricots
½ cup milk
125 g butter
½ cup caster sugar
3 eggs
2 cups self-raising flour
1 teaspoon grated lemon rind
¼ cup chopped walnuts

Why is a caterpillar like hot bread? Because it's the grub that makes the butterfly.

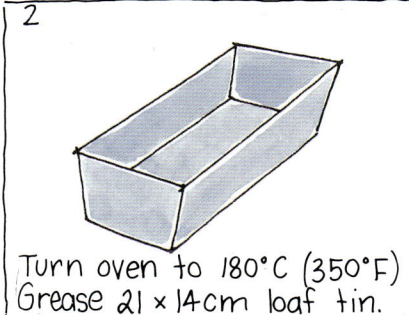

1. Put apricots + milk in a bowl. Set aside for 30 minutes.
2. Turn oven to 180°C (350°F). Grease 21 x 14cm loaf tin.
3. Beat butter + sugar well until smooth + creamy.
4. Add eggs. Beat them in very well.
5. Mix in apricots and milk. Stir in lemon rind.
6. Sift in flour. Mix it in well.
7. Spread it all evenly in the tin.
8. Sprinkle walnuts on top. Bake 55-60 minutes.

BIRTHDAY CAKE

Makes 1 x 20 cm cake

125 g butter
3/4 cup caster sugar
2 eggs, lightly beaten
1 teaspoon vanilla essence
2 cups self-raising flour
1/2 cup milk

1.  Turn oven to 180°C. Grease a 20cm round or heart-shaped tin. Line base with waxed paper.

2. Beat butter + sugar together until smooth + creamy.

3. Add eggs gradually. Beat well each time you add.

4. Add the vanilla essence. Beat it all well.

5. Gently fold in alternate spoonfuls of flour and milk until it's all added.

6. Stir until it's smooth. Spread evenly in tin. Bake 40 minutes.

7. Stick a skewer into the middle of the cake to check it's cooked — the skewer should come out clean.

8. Cool in tin 10 minutes, then turn out + cool completely on wire rack.
Mix 1½ cups icing sugar, 1 tablespoon butter - enough hot water to mix till smooth. Spread over cake. Decorate with jelly beans.

GIFTS FROM THE KITCHEN

You can make some really scrumptious gifts in your own kitchen — it's easy and it's fun. We have given you recipes for Fudge, Coconut Ice and Rum Truffles but you can also make gifts of any of the baked cakes, cookies and slices in the other chapters. Whenever a family birthday, celebration or Christmas comes around you can simply choose any of these favourite sweets or baked goodies to make and wrap.

Do take care when making any of the sweets as the mixtures that need cooking can become very hot.

To dress up your packages use clear or coloured cellophane, tissue paper, printed paper (or paint your own), small cardboard boxes, baskets or pretty tins. You'll also need brightly coloured ribbon and curling tape. Make your own labels from plain paper or cardboard and paint flowers or patterns and the person's name on them.

SOFT FUDGE

125 g plain milk chocolate
50 g butter
¼ cup evaporated milk
3 cups icing sugar

1. Lightly grease a 20 cm square tin.
2. Break up chocolate. Put in top of double boiler.
3. Add butter. Melt it all over gently simmering water.
4. Take it off the heat. Stir in evaporated milk
5. Sift in icing sugar. Mix it all well.
6. Press it all evenly into the tin.
7. Put in fridge until set.
8. Cut it into little squares.

Take melted chocolate and butter off heat, stir in evaporated milk.

Sift in the icing sugar and stir well to mix evenly.

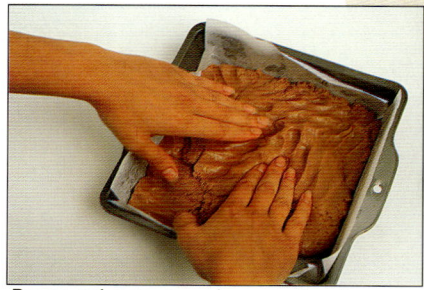

Press mixture evenly over the base of a square cake tin.

COCONUT ICE

2 cups icing sugar
3½ cups desiccated coconut
400 g can condensed milk
2-3 drops red food colouring

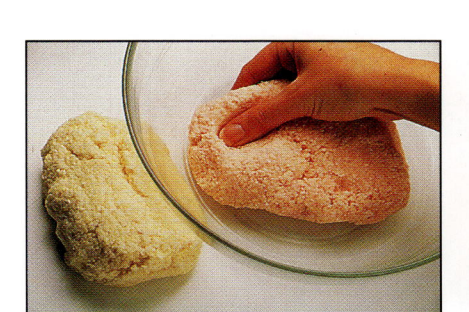

1. Lightly grease a 20 cm square cake tin. Line with baking paper.
2. Sift icing sugar into a large bowl, add half the coconut. Make a well in the centre and add the condensed milk.
3. Stir with a wooden spoon, then add remaining coconut and mix it in with your hands.
4. Put half the mixture into another bowl, add food colouring and knead until the colour is even.
5. Press the pink mixture into the prepared tin, then press the white mixture on top. Smooth with the back of a spoon.
6. Put the tin into the refrigerator for 1 hour, until mixture has set. Cut into small squares to serve.

Add the condensed milk.

Knead until the colour is even.

Cut into squares.

RUM TRUFFLES

1 cup cake crumbs
3 tablespoons caster sugar
70 g ground almonds
1 teaspoon cocoa
2 tablespoons grated chocolate
1 egg yolk
1 tablespoon rum
70 g packet chocolate hail
20 foil or paper sweet cases

1. Put crumbs, caster sugar and ground almonds in bowl.
2. Add cocoa, chocolate, egg yolk and rum.
3. Mix it well until it forms quite a smooth paste.
4. Divide it up into small teaspoonful lots.
5. Roll in cool, dry hands to form a ball.
6. Roll each ball in chocolate hail until covered.
7. Place each truffle in a foil or paper sweet case.
8. Put in a covered container in fridge until firm. They keep in fridge for about 10 days.

Divide rum truffle mixture evenly into small teaspoonfuls.

Roll each teaspoonful into small balls.

Roll each ball in chocolate hail until well covered.

CHAPTER EIGHT
COOKIES AND SLICES

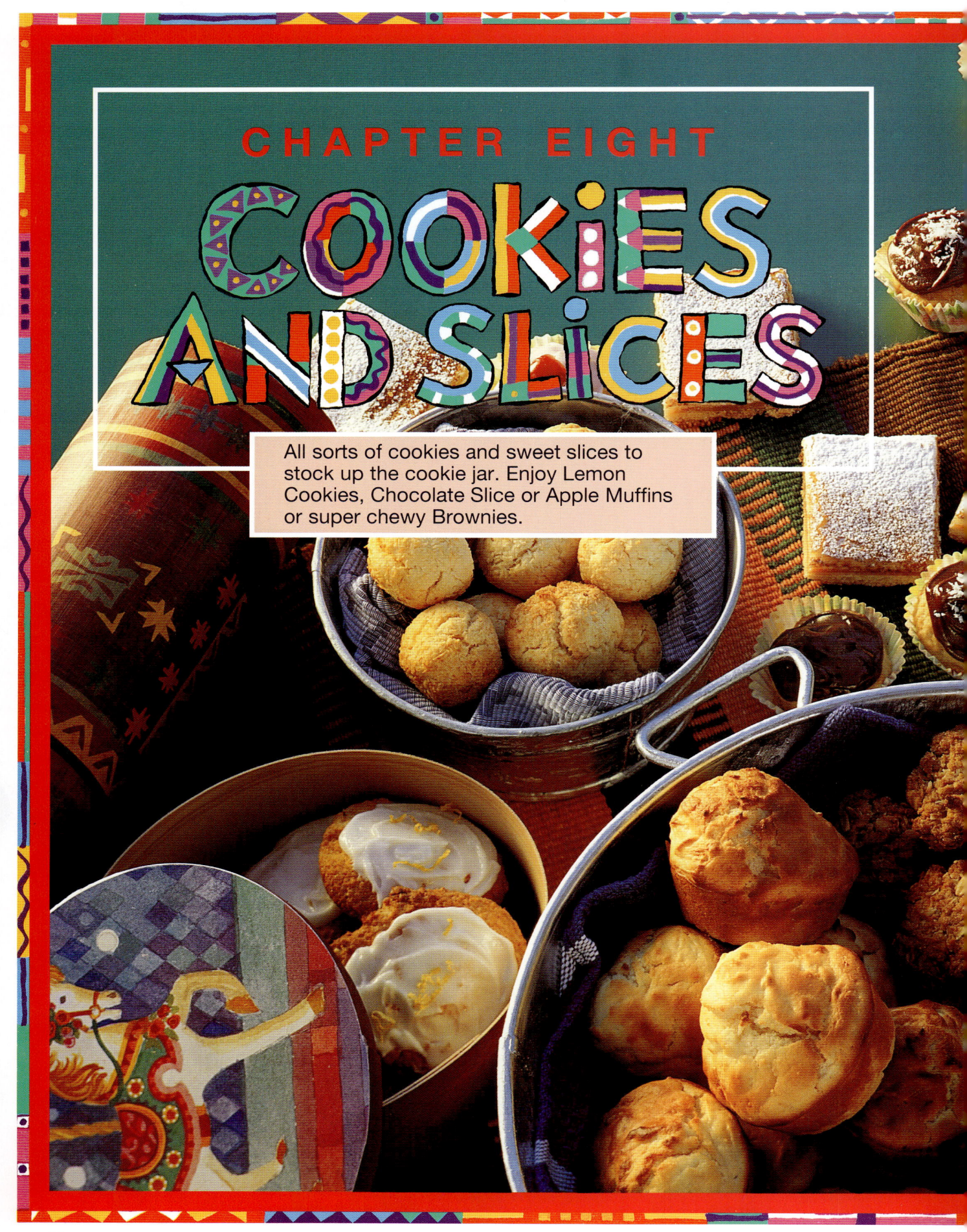

All sorts of cookies and sweet slices to stock up the cookie jar. Enjoy Lemon Cookies, Chocolate Slice or Apple Muffins or super chewy Brownies.

97

LEMON COOKIES

Makes about 48

¼ cup milk
1 teaspoon vinegar
125 g butter
¾ cup sugar
1 egg

1 teaspoon grated lemon rind
1¾ cups plain flour
1 teaspoon baking powder
¼ teaspoon salt

*Customer: May I have a newt-foot sandwich?
Sandwich-hand: Sorry, we're out of bread!*

1. Turn oven to 180°C (350°F). Mix milk + vinegar in cup. Set aside to turn sour.

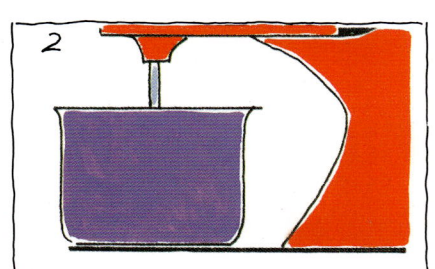

2. Beat butter, sugar, egg + lemon rind until smooth.

3. Sift in flour, baking powder and salt.

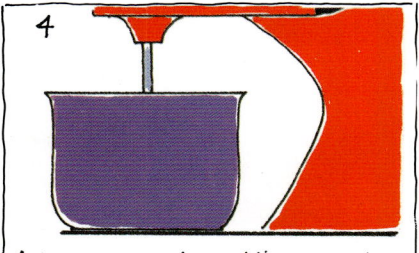

4. Add sour milk. Mix it all together well.

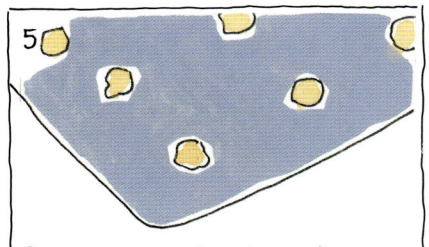

5. Put teaspoonful lots 5cm apart on an oven tray.

6. Bake 12 minutes or until golden (Bake 1 tray at a time)

7. Lift off tray. Cool on a wire rack. Makes about 48.

8. **Glaze:** Mix ½ cup icing sugar + 2 tablespoons lemon juice until mixed + smooth

Spread on hot cookie + leave until cold.

COCONUT COOKIES

Makes about 40

125 g butter
¾ cup caster sugar
1 egg
1 teaspoon vanilla essence
1 tablespoon white vinegar
1 cup desiccated coconut
2 cups self-raising flour
½ cup extra coconut

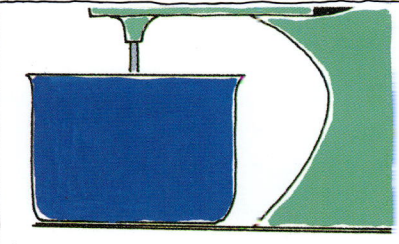

1. Turn oven to 180°C (350°F). Grease a baking tray.

2. Beat butter, sugar, egg + vanilla until smooth.

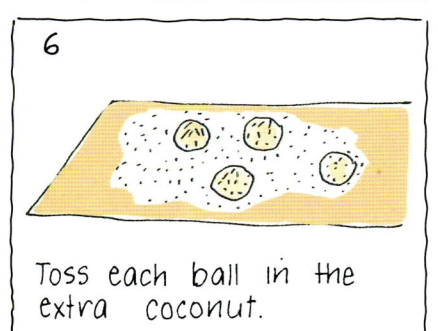

3. Stir vinegar into bowl.

4. Add coconut. Sift in flour. Mix well.

5. Roll heaped teaspoonsful of mixture into balls.

6. Toss each ball in the extra coconut.

7. Place 5 cm apart on the baking tray.

8. Bake 15 minutes or till golden. Cool on wire rack.

LEMON SLICE

Makes about 14 slices

100 g butter
¼ cup icing sugar
1 cup plain flour

TOPPING
2 eggs
2 tablespoons lemon juice
2 teaspoons grated lemon rind
1 cup caster sugar
2 tablespoons plain flour
½ teaspoon baking powder
1 tablespoon icing sugar

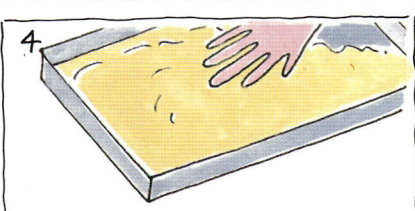

1. Turn oven to 180°C (350°F). Grease a 30 x 20cm tin.

2. Beat butter and icing sugar until smooth.

3. Sift in the 1 cup flour. Mix well to a smooth dough.

4. Press it evenly in the tin. Bake it for 20 minutes. Set aside to cool.

5. TOPPING: Beat the eggs well. Stir in lemon juice + lemon rind.

6. Sift in the caster sugar, the 2 tablespoons of flour + baking powder. Stir till mixed.

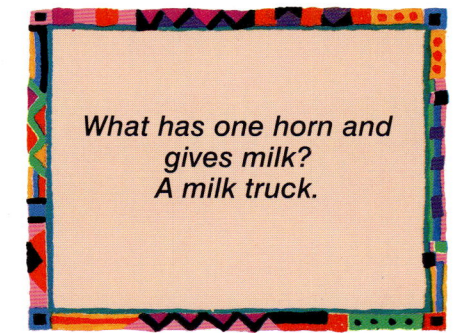

7. Pour it over the base. Bake again for 25 minutes.

8. Cool it. Sift icing sugar on top and cut into squares

What has one horn and gives milk?
A milk truck.

CHOCOLATE SLICE

Makes about 20 slices
250 g butter
1 cup caster sugar
3 tablespoons cocoa
1 egg, lightly beaten
2 cups desiccated coconut
2 cups cornflakes, crushed
2 cups plain flour
2 teaspoons baking powder
1 teaspoon vanilla essence

1. Turn oven to 180°C (350°F). Lightly grease 30 x 20cm tin.

2. Very gently melt the butter in a big pan.

3. Take it off the heat. Whisk in sugar and cocoa.

4. When sugar is dissolved add egg + stir in coconut + cornflakes.

5. Stir in flour, baking powder, and vanilla.

6. Stir it all well until it is completely mixed.

7. Press it all firmly into the tin, using your hands.

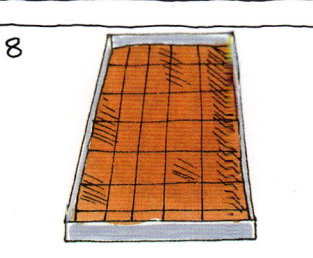

8. Bake for 20 minutes. When cold ice with chocolate icing, page 91.

BROWNIES

Makes about 20

200 g butter
½ cup cocoa
2 cups brown sugar
1 teaspoon imitation vanilla essence
1 cup plain flour
2 eggs
½ cup chopped walnuts

1. Turn oven to 180°C. Grease a 30 x 20 cm tin.

2. Put butter + cocoa in big pan. Melt gently. Don't boil it!

3. Add sugar and vanilla. Stir it really well.

4. Take off heat. Sift in the flour. Stir it in.

5. Add eggs. Beat them in really well.

6. Add chopped walnuts. Stir in.

7. Spread evenly in tin. Bake 20-25 minutes.

8. When cool, ice with chocolate icing, see page 91.

ANZAC BISCUITS

Makes about 25

- 2 cups rolled oats
- 2 cups plain flour
- 2 cups desiccated coconut
- 1½ cups caster sugar
- 250 g butter
- 4 tablespoons golden syrup
- 1 teaspoon baking soda
- 2 tablespoons boiling water

1. Turn oven to 160°C. Lightly grease oven trays.
2. Put oats, flour, coconut, sugar in big mixing bowl.
3. Melt butter + golden syrup in pan, stirring. Take off heat.
4. Mix baking soda + boiling water in a cup.
5. Add to melted butter in the pan. 
6.  Quickly add to big bowl. Mix it all well.
7. Roll tablespoonful lots into balls. Put on trays 5 cm apart.
8. Press lightly with fork. Bake 20 minutes — one tray at a time.

JAM SLICE

Makes about 24

125 g butter
½ cup caster sugar
1 egg
1½ cups plain flour
1 teaspoon baking powder
½ cup raspberry jam

TOPPING
1 egg
¼ cup caster sugar
1 cup desiccated coconut

1. Turn oven to 180°C. Grease a 20 cm square tin.

2. Put butter in big pan. Melt gently. Take off heat.

3. Add the ½ cup sugar + egg. Whisk it really well.

4. Sift in flour + baking powder. Mix it all well.

5. Spread evenly in tin. Spread jam evenly on top.

6. TOPPING: Put egg, ¼ cup sugar, coconut in bowl. Mix it all well.

7. Sprinkle + spread it evenly over.

8. Bake 30 minutes. Cool it in tin then slice.

105

APPLE MUFFINS

Makes about 12

1 cup wholemeal
   self-raising flour
1/2 cup brown sugar
1/2 cup oat bran
1/2 teaspoon cinnamon
1/4 cup chopped pecans
2 large green apples

1 egg
2/3 cup milk
60 g butter, melted

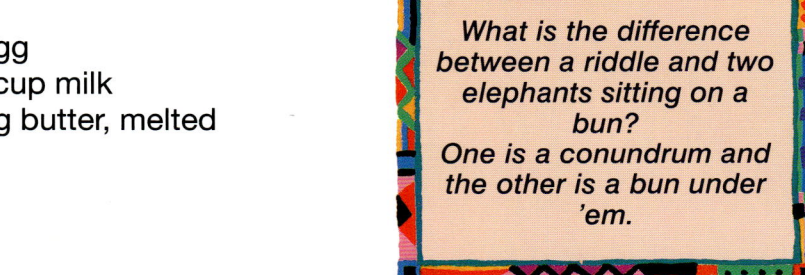

> What is the difference between a riddle and two elephants sitting on a bun?
> One is a conundrum and the other is a bun under 'em.

1. Turn oven to 220°C (425°F) Grease 12 muffin pans.

2. Sift flour into a bowl. Add sugar, oat bran, cinnamon + pecans.

3. Peel, then grate the apples. Stir them into the bowl.

4. Mix egg, milk and melted butter in a jug.

5. Add to bowl all at once. Stir with a fork.

6. Stir until just mixed. It is supposed to look lumpy.

7. Almost fill the pans with the batter.

8. Bake 15–20 minutes or until golden

Serve warm with butter + jam if you like

PATTY CAKES

Makes about 30

2 cups self-raising flour
¾ cup sugar
125 g soft butter
3 eggs
½ cup milk
½ teaspoon vanilla essence

1. Turn oven to 180°C (350°F). Set out 30 paper patty cases.

2. Sift flour, sugar into mixing bowl.

3. Add butter, eggs, milk and vanilla.

4. Beat it all very fast until it's quite smooth.

5. Fill patty cases until ¾ full with the mixture.

6. Bake for 15 minutes until golden.

7. Cool on a wire rack and then ice them.

8. ICING: Mix ¾ cup icing sugar, 1 teaspoon cocoa or 2-3 drops pink food colouring, 1 tablespoon butter with a little hot water until quite smooth. Ice the cakes.

STICKY BUNS

Makes 12

60 g butter ⎫
½ cup brown sugar ⎬ Step 1

2 tablespoons sultanas
2¼ cups plain flour
2 teaspoons baking powder
30 g butter (Step 3)

2 ripe bananas, mashed
½ cup milk
30 g butter, melted ⎫
2 tablespoons brown sugar ⎬ Step 6

What is put on a table, cut, but never eaten? A pack of cards.

1. Turn oven to 190°C (375°F). Melt the 60 g butter + the ½ cup brown sugar in a pan.

2. Stir in sultanas. Spoon mixture into base of 12 deep muffin pans.

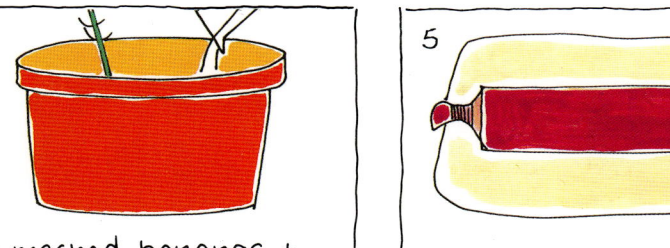

3. Sift flour + baking powder into bowl. Rub in the 30 g butter till it looks crumbly.

4. Add mashed bananas + milk. Mix it all quickly to form a soft dough.

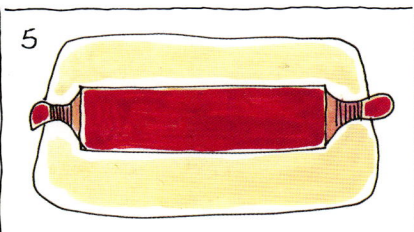

5. Knead it. Roll out on floured surface till it's 20 × 15 cm.

6. Spread melted butter over. Sprinkle brown sugar over.

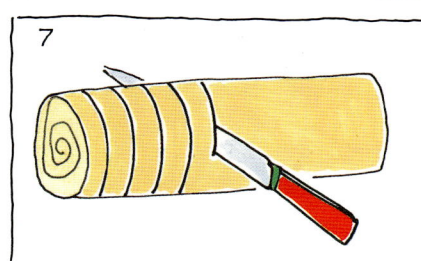

7. Firmly roll up (from long side). Cut neatly into 12 slices.

8. Put cut-side down in pans. Bake 12-15 minutes.

USEFUL INFORMATION

The recipes in this book are all thoroughly tested,
using standard metric measuring cups and spoons.
All cup and spoon measurements are level.
We have used eggs with an average weight of 60 g each
in all recipes.

Weights and Measures

In this book, metric measures and their imperial equivalents have been rounded out to the nearest figure that is easy to use. Different charts from different authorities vary slightly; the following are the measures we have used consistently throughout our recipes.

Oven Temperature Chart

	°C	°F
Very slow	120	250
Slow	150	300
Mod. slow	160	325
Moderate	180	350
Mod. hot	210 (190 gas)	425
Hot	240 (200 gas)	475
Very hot	260 (230 gas)	525

Length

Metric	Imperial
5 mm	¼ in
1 cm	½ in
2 cm	¾ in
2½ cm	1 in
5 cm	2 in
8 cm	3 in
10 cm	4 in
12 cm	5 in
15 cm	6 in
20 cm	8 in
25 cm	10 in
30 cm	12 in
46 cm	18 in
50 cm	20 in
61 cm	24 in

Cup and Spoon Measures

A basic metric cup set consists of 1 cup, ½ cup, ⅓ cup and ¼ cup sizes.

The basic spoon set comprises 1 tablespoon, 1 teaspoon, ½ teaspoon and ¼ teaspoon.

1 cup	250 ml (8 fl oz)
½ cup	125 ml (4 fl oz)
⅓ cup (4 tablespoons)	80 ml (2½ fl oz)
¼ cup (3 tablespoons)	60 ml (2 fl oz)
1 tablespoon	20 ml
1 teaspoon	5 ml
½ teaspoon	2.5 ml
¼ teaspoon	1.25 ml

Liquids

Metric	Imperial
30 ml	1 fl oz
60 ml	2 fl oz
100 ml	3½ fl oz
125 ml	4 fl oz (½ cup)
155 ml	5 fl oz
170 ml	5½ fl oz (⅔ cup)
200 ml	6½ fl oz
250 ml	8 fl oz (1 cup)
300 ml	9½ fl oz
375 ml	12 fl oz
410 ml	13 fl oz
470 ml	15 fl oz
500 ml	16 fl oz (2 cups)
600 ml	1 pt (20 fl oz)
750 ml	1 pt 5 fl oz (3 cups)
1 litre (1000 ml)	1 pt 12 fl oz (4 cups)

Dry Ingredients

Metric	Imperial
15 g	½ oz
30 g	1 oz
45 g	1½ oz
60 g	2 oz
75 g	2½ oz
100 g	3½ oz
125 g	4 oz
155 g	5 oz
185 g	6 oz
200 g	6½ oz
250 g	8 oz
300 g	9½ oz
350 g	11 oz
375 g	12 oz
400 g	12½ oz
425 g	13½ oz
440 g	14 oz
470 g	15 oz
500 g	1 lb (16 oz)
750 g	1 lb 8 oz
1 kg (1000 g)	2 lb

Glossary

capsicum = sweet pepper
cornflour = cornstarch

INDEX

Anzac Biscuits 103
apples
   Apple Muffins 106
   Apple Pudding 74
   Apple Turnovers 84
   Baked Apples 75
Apricot Loaf 92
bananas
   Banana Cake 90
   Banana Delicious 77
   Banana Milkshake 21
basil, in Tomato Salad 29
Bean Salad 26
beef
   Beef Casserole 46
   Macaroni Mince 58
   Meat Loaf 47
   Savoury Pie 55
Big Pizza 59
Birthday Cake 93
Boiled Eggs 51
bread *see also* buns, toast
   Ham and Cheese Bread 64
breakfast 50
Brownies 102
buns
   Pizza Snack 18
   Sticky Buns 108
cabbage, in Coleslaw 28
cakes
   Apricot Loaf 92
   Banana Cake 90
   Birthday Cake 93
   Carrot Cake 88
   Chocolate Cake 89
   Fudge Cake 91
   Patty Cakes 107
   Pineapple Cake 70
   Upside-Down Cake 76
capsicum, in Mixed Salad 30
Carrot Cake 88
cheese
   Cheese and Potato Bake 68
   Cheese Snack 14
   Cheese Toast 63
   Ham and Cheese Bread 64
   Pizza Snacks 18
chicken
   Chicken and Corn Soup 62
   Chicken and Ginger 39
   Chicken and Vegetables 40
   Chicken Wings 38
   Creamy Chicken 65
   Grilled Chicken 41
Choco Banana Split 83
chocolate icing 91
Chocolate Cake 89
Chocolate Crunch 71
Chocolate Slice 101
Chocolate Sundae 82
Cinnamon Toast 15
Coconut Cookies 99
Coconut Ice 95
Coffee Float 20

Coleslaw 28
cookies
   Coconut Cookies 99
   Lemon Cookies 98
Cordial, Lemon 22
corn, in Chicken and Corn Soup 62
cornflakes
   Chocolate Crunch 71
   Fruit Crumble 79
Corn Fritters 34
cream, in Pavlova Roll 69
cream cheese, in Onion Dip 17
Creamy Chicken 65
Crumble, Fruit 79
eggs
   Boiled Eggs 51
   Pavlova Roll 69
   Spanish Omelette 66
fish
   Fish Cakes 44
   Salmon Mornay 42
   Tuna Loaf 43
Flummery, Fruit 85
Fruit Crumble 79
Fruit Cup 50
fruit juice 50
Fruit Punch 23
Fudge, Soft 94
Fudge Cake 91
Garlic Toast 16
ginger, in Chicken and Ginger 39
grapefruit juice 50
green beans, in Bean Salad 26
Grilled Chicken 41
ham
   Ham and Cheese Bread 64
   Ham and Pineapple 49
ice cream
   Choco Banana Split 83
   Chocolate Sundae 82
   Coffee Float 20
icing
   chocolate 91
   lemon 88
Jam Slice 104
kidney beans, in Bean Salad 26
Lemon Cookies 98
Lemon Cordial 22
lemon icing 88
Lemon Slice 100
Macaroni Bake 57
Macaroni Mince 58
mayonnaise, in Potato Salad 27
Meat Loaf 47
milk
   Banana Milkshake 21
   Coffee Float 20
Mixed Salad 30
Muffins, Apple 106
mushrooms, in Mixed Salad 30
Omelette, Spanish 66
onions
   Onion Dip 17
   Onion Tart 54

Onion and Tomato 33
orange juice 50
   Fruit Punch 23
Pancakes 78
pasta
   cooking pasta 9
   Macaroni Bake 57
   Macaroni Mince 58
pastry
   Apple Turnovers 84
   Onion Tart 54
   Sausage Pie 56
Patty Cakes 107
Pavlova Roll 69
peaches, in Fruit Crumble 79
pies *see* pastry
pineapple
   Fruit Crumble 79
   Ham and Pineapple 49
   Pineapple Cake 70
pizza
   Big Pizza 59
   Pizza Snacks 18
potatoes
   Cheese and Potato Bake 68
   Fish Cakes 44
   mashed 9
   Potato Salad 27
pumpkin
   Glazed Pumpkin 32
   mashed 9
Punch, Fruit 23
rice
   cooking rice 9
   Savoury Pie 55
   Savoury Rice 35
Rum Truffles 95
salads 26-30
salami, in Pizza Snacks 18
Salmon Mornay 42
Sausage Pie 56
Savoury Pie 55
Savoury Rice 35
Soft Fudge 94
Soup, Chicken and Corn 62
Spanish Omelette 66
Steamed Pudding 80
Sticky Buns 108
sweet corn, in Chicken and Corn Soup 62
Sweet and Sour Meatballs 48
tarts *see* pastry
Tea 51
Toast 51
   Cheese Toast 14
   Cinnamon Toast 15
   Garlic Toast 16
tomatoes
   Onion and Tomato 33
   Mixed Salad 30
   Tomato Salad 29
Truffles, Rum 95
Tuna Loaf 43
Upside-Down Cake 76
zucchini, in Mixed Salad 30

This edition published in 2010 by Bay Books, an imprint of Murdoch Books Pty Limited,
Pier 8/9, 23 Hickson Road, Millers Point, NSW 2000, Australia.
Phone: +61 2 8220 2000 Fax: +61 2 8220 2558
www.murdochbooks.com.au

Murdoch Books UK Limited
Erico House, 6th Floor North, 93–99 Upper Richmond Road, Putney, London SW15 2TG
Phone: +44 (0) 20 8785 5995 Fax: +44 (0) 20 8785 5985
www.murdochbooks.co.uk

Chief Executive: Juliet Rogers

Publisher: Lynn Lewis **Senior Designer and Cover Designer:** Heather Menzies **Designer:** Michele Lichtenberger
Photographers: Jo Filshie, Reg Morrison (steps) **Production:** Joan Beal

National Library of Australia Cataloguing-in-Publication Data

Title: Kids' Cookbook
ISBN 978-1-74266-182-7 (pbk.)
Notes: Includes index
Subjects: Cooking – Juvenile literature
Dewey Number: 641.5123

First published in 1991. This edition published in 2010.
Printed by Sing Cheong Printing Co Ltd. PRINTED IN CHINA.

Copyright © Text, design, photography and illustrations Murdoch Books 1991.
All rights reserved. No part of this publication may be reproduced, stored in a retrieval system or transmitted in any form or by any means, electronic, mechanical, photocopying, recording or otherwise without the prior written permission of the publisher.